Space to Create

A Writer's View on the
Housing Crisis

Ben Irvine

Oldspeak Publishing.

First published in 2018.

All content © Ben Irvine 2018.

With special thanks to Rebecca Watts for her assistance.

All references and links to sources are available from
www.benirvine.co.uk

I told my mother, "Mother, I must leave you.
Preserve my room, but do not shed a tear.
Should rumour of a shabby ending reach you,
It was half my fault, and half the atmosphere".

Leonard Cohen, from 'The Traitor'

1.

A few months ago I purchased a house – with a great sense of relief. Britain is in the grip of an unrelenting housing crisis, and I've spent the last decade caught up in it. Before I become complacent, I want to reflect on what it has been like being a young person in a developed country where one of life's necessities has become a scarce resource. I hope that this book, which is a sort of memoir of the housing crisis, will open a few people's eyes.

Young people are disproportionately bearing the brunt of the crisis. Many have been priced out of owning or even renting their own home. Recent statistics show that the proportion of young adults living with their parents in the UK is larger than ever; one in four adults aged 18 to 34 still lives under the same roof as mum and dad. That's a rise from 2.7 million to 3.4 million in two decades. A study by the homelessness charity Shelter has suggested that, based on current trends, the proportion of young adults living with their parents will exceed 50% within a gen-eration. And, of course, homelessness is a growing problem in the UK. There are currently more than 300,000 homeless people in Britain. One in five young people report having stayed temporarily with friends or relatives – 'sofa surfing', as it's called – because of a lack of permanent accommodation. Nearly one in ten young people report having sofa surfed for more than a month.

Admittedly, in some ways I'm not a standard example of a young person. Though I attended a state school in a working-class area of North East London, I ended up completing a PhD in Philosophy at Cambridge University, and now I'm an internationally published writer. (And – ahem – I'm not very young anymore). If I had wanted to sail clear of the housing crisis by cashing in on my education and climbing through the ranks of a professional career, I suppose I could have done. Instead, I chose to prioritise my writing career. For almost ten years, I have supported myself through various low-paid evening jobs, and I continue to do so. In that sense, you could argue I've been something of a housing crisis tourist: I have made life hard for myself voluntarily. But actually I think stories like mine are an overlooked aspect of the crisis. Almost all aspiring artists – writers, painters, illustrators, musicians, magicians, actors, dancers, comedians, or whatever – will have to 'slum it' at some point in their careers, especially early on. The same goes for aspiring entrepreneurs, or any other creative type of person. For creative people, keeping costs down is part of the process of success. Unfortunately, with housing costs skyrocketing, keeping costs down isn't as easy as it used to be. The housing crisis has made it harder for young people to pursue creative careers.

Another reason the housing crisis has been particularly hard on artists and entrepreneurs is that creative people are notorious for needing their 'space'. In the physical sense, space has become increasingly hard to come by. Recent statistics reveal a 'surge' in overcrowded homes; in England and Wales more than three million people now live in a house with at least five other individuals. Granted, some people enjoy communal living. But creative people often prefer to live alone, because physical space is a precondition of the 'mental space' they need; pursuing a creative project requires a lot of deep thinking, imagining, planning and organising. Alas, mental space is obliterated by distraction and disturbance, and, in a shared house, distractions and disturbances abound. Whether it's housemates talking on their mobile phones, housemates Skyping, housemates watching TV, housemates playing music or video games, housemates having loud sex, housemates getting up early in the morning, housemates coming home drunk late at night, or housemates just *being there...* shared living drags creative people down to the lowest common denominator of unfocusedness. When George Orwell wrote his masterpiece *Nineteen Eighty-Four*, he took himself off to a cottage on the remote Scottish island of Jura. He wanted, he said, to become 'ungetatable'. Any creative person will know exactly what Orwell meant.

If this all sounds like middle-class moaning, let me explain that there is another aspect to my experience of being a writer during the housing crisis. Being chronically poor has given me an insight into many topics that I studiously avoided during my education. While I was studying philosophy, I never dreamed of what life is like for people outside of the so-called 'elites'. But now I know what it's like to survive on a low wage, and to live in cheap lodgings (as, indeed, Orwell himself knew). As a result, my sympathies have changed beyond recognition – mostly, but not always, in favour of the proverbial 'man in the street'. I've become wary of intellectuals. The trouble with intelectuals is that, in their arrogance, one of the countless things they are ignorant of is how much damage their ideas can do. Bad ideas lead to bad social norms and bad governance. The housing crisis, I now believe, derives predominantly from bad ideas – ideas that urgently need to be challenged with a heavy dose of reality. Sometimes it takes a tourist like me to state the obvious.

Or, indeed, a refugee – of sorts. The house I bought is located in a former mining village in the North East of England, an economically deprived region that has remained on the periphery of the housing bubble that has engulfed the rest of the UK. My house cost me a twentieth of what a similar dwelling would have cost in London, where I grew up. I'm very fond of the North East – I did my undergraduate and Master's degrees at Durham University – so my move back here hasn't been too much of a wrench. But the fact is, I'm a housing crisis refugee. I've left my family down south, because living anywhere near London isn't economically viable for me. In this, I'm far from alone. Most of my school friends have moved away from London, because even people with decent jobs are struggling in the capital. Native Londoners are abandoning their city in droves. I haven't really escaped the housing crisis. I'm running away from it every day.

Sometimes I miss London. Well, I miss the London of my childhood. Since then, our capital city has turned into something I can't relate to at all. Over the last decade, I've come to see London as an emblem of the conditions – economic, governmental, social, political and intellectual – that have caused the housing crisis. People say you should never look back in anger. I guess they're right. But looking back in judgement is another thing entirely.

2.

My own personal housing crisis began in late 2007, when I was in the final stages of my PhD. Any scholar will tell you that this is a stressful time. You've got 80,000 words of your thesis to complete, along with thousands of footnotes to check. Then, once you've submitted your thesis, you'll have to wait several months until your verbal examination takes place, after which – typically – your examiners will insist that you make numerous alterations to your thesis, which may require a few more months' work. Meanwhile, you'll probably have run out of money. Doctoral funding usually lasts three years, but researching and writing a PhD usually takes longer than that. Mine took almost four years (which is about average).

Right after I submitted my PhD thesis, I started working as a bar tender in my college bar in the evenings. During the daytimes, I tutored a few undergraduates and I read lots of philosophy books; you have to be prepared to answer some pretty abstruse questions in your verbal exam. At the same time, I had to find somewhere to live outside of college. Up until this point, my college – King's College, Cambridge – had been in the habit of offering rented accommodation to PhD candidates awaiting their verbal exams. However, things had recently changed. The financial management of my college had largely been turned over to the 'catering and hospitality' department. Basically this meant that King's was increasingly being used as a conference centre and hotel. Week after week, the student bar was full of drunken wedding guests and corporate parties, while rooms were being rented out to these various visitors. I don't generally disapprove of any educational establishment entrepreneurially making money. But the way my college was making money was a sign of the times. Because of the housing crisis, real estate was becoming a highly lucrative asset. Presumably, my college – or, rather, the people running it – had concluded that there was a lot more money to made from renting out rooms to party guests and conference attendees than to its own graduate students.

Still, I was 28 years old; the chord needed to be cut. I had been cloistered within higher education for a decade. I knew I needed to face up to life. I knew this theoretically as well as instinctively. Throughout my studies, I had come to suspect that much of academic philosophy consists in a sort of reality-avoidance scheme for neurotic intellectuals. In the final chapter of my PhD thesis, I argued that most philosophers, and many other intellectuals, hypochondriacally make a problem out of life itself. These 'philosophical hypochondriacs', as I called them, conjure up life-denying theories and ideologies to distract themselves from their own existence and from their respon-sibilities. In the process, philosophical hypochondriacs cynically drum up support by insisting that their position above the fray gives them the intellectual and moral insight to be able to provide guidance and leadership to the rest of the population. Having come to this realisation, I was more than ready to broaden my own horizons.

Moreover, for a long time I had harboured positive expectations of the sort of life I would lead after my studies. When I was a teenager, one of my sisters had a long-term boyfriend who was a poet. I always looked up to him (and for good reason: he went on to win the T. S. Eliot prize). While I was an undergraduate, he and I became friends, and in the ensuing years I visited him many times at his home. In the early stages of his career, he lived in a northern town where he worked part-time in a bookshop. I don't know how much he paid in rent – we've lost touch now – but I remember that his job enabled him to have a whole house to himself, where he worked intensely on his craft. Scattered throughout the house were scraps of paper with lines of poetry scrawled on them. Empty coffee cups abounded. His house even had space for a study room, in which his books were piled high in a heroic jumble. I was inspired. I remember thinking that one day I wanted to live like that. If I ended up impoverished it wouldn't matter, so long as I could fill my days with creativity, in a bohemian house just like the one my sister's boyfriend lived in.

Little did I know that in the decade following my PhD my life would gradually sink into chaos, conflict and dismay, largely due to the places I lived in and the people I lived with. My dreams of a creative life were in jeopardy from the start. Between 1997 and 2007 – which was the period of my higher education, a period encompassing my A-levels, undergraduate degree, Master's degree and PhD – average house prices in the UK more than trebled. As a result, when I went looking for a place to live in Cambridge in 2007 I had a rude awakening. I found that most of the rooms on the rental market cost at least £400 per month (taking bills into account), while most of the single-occupancy flats or houses were at least twice as expensive. Naturally, the cheapest rooms were the least attractive; they were tiny, or noisy, or dirty, or came with disreputable housemates. To put this situation in perspective, I was working around 30 hours a week behind the bar, and earning around £750 a month in total. The monthly rent that I would have to pay felt like a mountain to climb. I realised I was going to struggle to afford a suitable room in Cambridge, never mind a house of my own.

I needed a plan B, and luckily there was an obvious choice – well, obvious to me. I asked my dad if I could borrow his camper van, and he kindly agreed. Thus, I moved my stuff into my first post-university home: a rickety old yellow Volkswagen Combi, which I parked at the end of a quiet street in Cambridge. It was late November, and it was cold, but I didn't mind. At night I wore lots of layers and a woolly hat, and I slept beneath two duvets. Every day, I went into my college to take a shower in the graduate block. Some nights I even managed to persuade my girlfriend to sleep in the van with me. Those were happy days.

Unfortunately, about a month in, the door fell off the van. Right off. I flung it open one morning and it clattered onto the pavement, like a clanking metaphor for my life. Looking back, I don't know why I didn't arrange to have the door fixed. I was lacking in initiative, I suppose, not to mention a sense of responsibility. And – to be fair – I was worried that even with an airtight van I would freeze to death when the winter set in. So, with the wind whirling through the gaping hole in the bodywork, I drove my dad's wounded van down the M11 and deposited it blithely at my parents' house in London. Then I returned to Cambridge to restart my search for a place to live.

Without delay, I took a room in a flat in the centre of town for £420 a month. I sub-let the room from a German couple; they were academics who were returning to Germany for a while. The other room in the flat was tenanted by an Irish PhD student. I got on fine with him. The only problem was that my room was ludicrously noisy. It was located directly above a kebab shop that was open every night until 4am. Drunken students would pour out of the town's nightclubs then queue up for a greasy bite to eat. There was a carnival atmosphere in the queue. I struggled to sleep while people whooped and sang and shouted and argued and fought in the street below. Here I learned my first lesson in how to survive the housing crisis: ear plugs are essential.

I soon realised I was facing a dilemma – a dilemma that would hang over me for many years. I wanted to pursue a creative life, and in order to do this I needed a half-decent place to live. However, in order to afford a half-decent place to live I would have to get a well-paid job, a job that would be so time-consuming and energy-draining that I would struggle to pursue my creative projects.

Actually, I was facing a trilemma. There was a third option: I could get a job as an academic. In theory, academia was the perfect solution. As an academic, I could pursue a creative life *and* afford a decent place to live. However, for various reasons, an academic career wasn't likely to work out for me. One problem was that I felt alienated from professional philosophy.

I didn't want to continue studying philosophical problems that I knew were pseudo-problems. On the contrary, I wanted, as a writer, to expose those 'problems' for what they were. Moreover, my academic colleagues were hardly likely to support me in such a project. Tutoring undergraduates was one thing, but getting a lectureship or a research job in academia was something else entirely; I would need to write several peer-reviewed publications, and do a lot of networking and reputation-building. Neither my heart nor my head was in it. My outlook was further darkened by the fact that my PhD supervisor, the wonderful Professor Peter Lipton, died suddenly of a heart attack a few days after I submitted my thesis. He was only 52. Professor Lipton was the closest thing I had to an ally in academia. His last words to me were: "Ben, you are brilliant. But you are an iconoclast. There should be funding for someone like you, but there isn't."

A final reason I didn't pursue an academic career in early 2008 was that I had a few health problems at the time. Individually, these problems were minor, but cumulatively they were dragging me down. I decided the best course of action was to take the financial pressure off while I prepared for my verbal exam and sorted out my health (I needed to have my tonsils and two infected wisdom teeth removed, and an operation to fix a broken nose that had healed problematically). So I quit my room in Cambridge and moved back to my parents' house in London. I was awarded my PhD in the spring of 2008. Then I started looking for a decent job in the capital.

3.

What can I say that hasn't already been said about living with your parents when you're an adult? At unnaturally close quarters, the relationship between parents and their adult children becomes anachronistic: adult children see their parents through the eyes of peers not acolytes; parents see their adult children through the eyes of warders not supporters. From both sides, harsh judgments and criticisms ensue, sharpened by the righteousness of love. Let's just say that when I found a decent job and moved out of my parents' house soon afterwards, I was mightily relieved – and I'm sure my parents were too.

Thankfully, finding a well-paid job didn't take me long, despite the Great Recession raging all around me. When I was a teenager, I had completed a week's work experience at Brent Council. In 2008, I contacted a man I had met while I was there. He was now a senior member of staff for the Council. I asked him if there were any job openings in his office. There were. Soon afterwards, I applied for, and was offered, a role as a 'Project Officer' in Brent Council's housing department.

I went into the job with idealistic hopes that I could 'make a difference'. Brent Council, like every local authority in the UK, provides welfare services to people who are 'in need'. Some of these needy people are given money in the form of various 'benefits' – child benefit, unemployment benefit, disability benefit, and so on. Some are provided with council-owned housing; others are given money for renting accommodation in the private sector. At the time, I didn't question this idea of 'need'. It seemed obvious enough that the motley assortment of people who came through our doors were needy. It never occurred to me to ask *how* some of them came to be that way.

It didn't take me long, however, to question the value of my own contribution to the whole set-up – or, indeed, that of anyone else in my office. None of us did much other than drink coffee, fiddle with spreadsheets, generate pat responses to complaints letters, write reports, email each other, and occasionally answer the telephone. The lady who sat opposite me spent almost all her time playing solitaire on her computer. Whenever anyone interrupted her game, she would sigh and tut. The whole office was pervaded by an atmosphere of impotence and disillusionment. There were so many people in need, yet no matter how much manpower we had at our disposal – or, indeed, *because* we had so much manpower at our disposal – we never seemed to have enough resources. We were reduced to sitting around complaining about the failings of 'the system' and 'the government'.

On one occasion, I attended a meeting where the Director of our unit was outlining the scale of the perpetual challenge we faced. Naively, I raised my hand and asked a question that seemed obvious: "If this isn't working, is there another way?" You could've heard a pin drop. The other staff members cleared their throats, analysed their finger nails, looked out the window, and shuffled in their chairs. The Director said "hmmmm" and swiftly moved on to the next agenda item.

I, too, rapidly became disillusioned. My lowest point in the job was a moment of nightmarish epiphany, in which my manager's true priorities became clear to me. He had asked me to produce a magazine to promote the Council's 'Low Cost Home Ownership' programme. I enjoyed the actual process of creating the magazine, and I was proud and excited when I was asked to take some of the printed copies to an event where a local politician would be present. I showed the politician the magazine and, flicking through the pages, he was evidently impressed by all the pictures of shiny happy people in front of shiny new houses. But this only made me more furious at what happened next. The very next day my manager told me to throw the rest of the magazines in the bin. "No one will read them now", he said. "The Councillor has seen them; you've done your job". I couldn't believe it. I was wasting my efforts – literally.

Meanwhile, things weren't going well with my own housing situation. I had moved into a small room in a shared house in Kilburn. The rent was £575 per month (plus a one-off 'admin' fee of £175 to the estate agent). I had found the room via an online advert, in which the household was described as 'sociable'; that sounded alright to me. I soon learned my second lesson in surviving the housing crisis: never, ever take a room in a household that is advertised as 'sociable'. Not unless you want to live with determinedly anti-social people.

My housemates were two females in their mid-twenties. One was a lawyer; the other was a marketer. To them, 'sociable' meant getting drunk (or – for the marketer – taking drugs). It also meant talking incessantly, but always *at* a person, never *with* a person. The more intoxicated the women were, the more verbally incontinent they became. One night they held a dinner party, to which I was invited as a member of their sociable household. The dinner party consisted of five heavily intoxicated attendees talking louder and louder, in long boring bursts of waffle that ended only when one of the attendees interrupted another's long boring burst with a long boring burst of their own. My contribution was to sit and watch their yapping heads, with a growing sense of dismay. I love conversation. But this wasn't *con*versation. At best, it was versation.

My housemates' selfishness as communicators was reflected in their general behaviour as housemates. They were noisy – especially in the mornings. The lawyer got up at 6am on weekdays. She was woken by a radio alarm clock, which she would leave on for an hour while she marched around the house, slamming doors and clonking in the kitchen and bathroom. Then the marketer would get up and do the same for another hour. They both knew that I didn't need to get up until 8am, but they didn't care. At night, they often watched TV till late, especially at the weekends. Or they guffawed and shrieked their way through a bottle of wine. Or they blathered into their mobile phones in the communal spaces. In this kind of atmosphere, even a sturdy old Victorian brick house seems to have paper walls. I should have asked my housemates to be quieter. These days I'm more confident, and I would do so. But I felt as though I was a guest in their house – a guest, moreover, who had been forewarned that they were 'sociable'. If I went to bed before them, sometimes I would make a big show of saying "goodnight" in the hope that they'd take the hint. They didn't. With my earplugs in, I learned to live a muffled version of the life I had hoped for.

There was only one occasion when I felt I connected on a personal level with one of my housemates – and I rapidly regretted it. I was sitting in the living room with the lawyer one evening, chatting. For once, I was actually chatting with her, as opposed to getting chatted at. We were talking about mental illness. We both suffered from anxiety, it turned out. While we were exchanging stories, and sharing our worries, the lawyer confided in me that her mother had died of cancer a few years previously. I said I was very sorry to hear it, and I asked her how she was coping now. She replied that she had gradually come to terms with the loss, but her biggest worry was that she herself would get cancer one day; sometimes, she said, she felt she was going crazy with the worry.

When you hear such a sad tale, it's hard to know what to say. I decided to say this: "I don't think you're crazy for worrying about that, but I'm sure you'll be absolutely fine."

Not the best response, I'll grant you. But anyway, I didn't get to finish my glib verdict. I got as far as "I don't think you're crazy for worrying about that…" when the lawyer interrupted, sharply.

"What do you mean?"

I had dug myself a hole, and I stupidly tried to dig my way out.

"I mean, what I'm saying is, you're not worrying unreasonably. You're not crazy."

"Are you saying I'm going to get cancer?"

"Oh, no. I'm saying I can understand why you're worried. I'm sure you'll be absol…"

"Fuck you, you fucking bastard."

And thus she stomped out of the room, slammed the door behind her, and didn't speak to me for two months. During that period I repeatedly tried to apologise, but every time I spoke to her she would immediately stomp out again then disappear into her bedroom. I tried to discuss the situation with the other girl, the marketer, to see if she could help smooth things over, but she shot back "I'm not getting involved", in a slightly aggressive manner that made it clear where her sympathies lay. Faced with my new status as *persona non grata* in my own home, I felt uncomfortable being there. I started avoiding the house. I often stayed over at my friends' places – not exactly sofa surfing, but not exactly not sofa surfing either. During this time, of course, I continued to pay the rent.

Eventually, the situation came to a head. When I went into the kitchen one evening to cook some dinner, the lawyer turned to stomp out, as usual. But this time I decided enough was enough. I called after her: "You're being childish."

She replied: "I've asked all my friends, and they all said that what you said was one of the most horrible things they've ever heard."

"I asked my friends, too," I replied, "and they said you're overreacting."

"That's because you're a fucking bastard," she concluded.

Clearly, I wasn't going to climb out of this hole any day soon. I needed to find a new place to live.

4.

First of all, however, I needed to try to extract myself from the contract I had signed for the room. This is another seldom remarked-on aspect of the housing crisis. The demand for decent accommodation is so high these days that estate agents can get away with tying customers into draconian contracts. Having signed up to a one-year commitment, I couldn't leave the house until a replacement tenant had been found. Luckily, my estate agent was sympathetic to my predicament, and he helped me find a suitable candidate without much delay. I suppose there's no shortage of people wanting to live in a sociable household. I was also lucky that my estate agent didn't hit me with lots of extra fees on my departure. I have heard horror stories of tenants who, on departing, have been charged hundreds of pounds in the name of 'checkout inspection fees' and 'professional cleaning fees', along with various other (extortionate) charges for scuffs, marks and new lightbulbs.

Soon enough I found another room, in a flat in Brondesbury. I shared the flat with a live-in landlady – a successful young journalist – and another female tenant, who worked in a bank. They were both nice people, although mostly we kept ourselves to ourselves. The room cost an eye-watering £850 per month, but on a rolling contract – so I could leave whenever I liked. The flat, which was located on the top floor of a grand old apartment block, was lovely, and the atmosphere was quiet and friendly. You get what you pay for, I guess. For a little while, I felt settled. Through my job, I had enough money to live comfortably, and I started paying off my student debts. It felt good to be back in London. On work days, I got into the habit of riding my bicycle through leafy backstreets to my office near Wembley Stadium, and on weekends I socialised with my old friends, including some of my university friends who had moved down to the capital. Some weekends, I went exploring on my bike. I enjoyed discovering a side of London that I had never seen when I was growing up.

But I wasn't living the creative life I had dreamed about. I wanted to write books, and that wasn't going to happen when I was working full-time. Creativity-wise, I'm a morning person. Each morning I have a window of opportunity of about seven hours during which I'm fresh and ready for creative work. After that, invariably, a peasouper of a mental fog descends on me, and I have no desire (let alone ability) to be creative. Sometimes I get a second creative wind at about 8pm for an hour or two, but not reliably. I knew I was never going to write a book when I was spending my daily window of creative opportunity staring out of an actual window in a dreary office block in Brent. I needed to make changes.

My colleagues in Brent knew I aspired to become a writer. Therefore they were unsurprised when I handed in my notice after a year in the job. They thought I was crazy though. I suppose what I was planning was risky: I had decided to start a business. I figured that I could work on my business during the afternoons and evenings, leaving my mornings free for writing philosophy. I would live off the money the business made, thus self-funding my writing. Obviously, if this plan was going to have any chance of success, I needed a strong idea for a business.

Inspired by my many bike rides through London, and by my experience of producing the housing magazine for Brent Council, my idea was to create a free cycling magazine that would target an audience of *potential cyclists* as opposed to existing cyclists. I figured that cycling was a massive growth industry in the UK, and to my knowledge there weren't any publications that promoted bicycles and bicycle-related products to would-be cyclists – the very people who were fuelling the growth in the industry. This seemed to me a huge gap in the market. If I could help retailers reach would-be cyclists, I could potentially sell a lot of advertising space in the magazine. I also planned to sell bespoke versions of the magazine to local authorities in London and beyond. Local authorities are always keen to promote cycling; I figured that a specially tailored local version of my magazine would make it much easier and cheaper for them to do so.

I named the magazine *Cycle Lifestyle*. By most measures, it was a success. It was profitable every year, peaking in the fourth year when I made over £10,000. It gave me a platform from which to start a major (ongoing) campaign that I am passionate about – the London Cycle Map Campaign, which is calling for a Tube-style map and network of signed cycle routes in the capital. And I suppose the magazine persuaded a few people to get back on their bikes, which is surely a good thing. Moreover, from a personal point of view, running the magazine did indeed give me the opportunity to begin writing popular philosophy. While I was working on *Cycle Lifestyle*, I snatched time in the mornings to work on various philosophy projects, including founding a new journal, the *Journal of Modern Wisdom*. The magazine even helped me get my first book deal. I was approached by a publisher, Ivy Press; they were looking for someone to write a book about philosophy and cycling. I eagerly accepted the offer, and my first book, *Einstein and the Art of Mindful Cycling*, was born – out of a strange fusion of entrepreneurship, serendipity, my burgeoning experience as a writer of popular philosophy, and the fact that I happened to be reading a biography of Einstein at the time when Ivy Press approached me.

In its early days, *Cycle Lifestyle* was mightily helped by the fact that not long after I left my job in Brent my former boss contacted me to offer me some work as a consultant. On the face of it, this was ludicrous. I had worked in the public sector for only a year, so I was hardly someone worth consulting. But they needed someone to write a one-off strategy report – presumably some councillor somewhere needed an impressive new publication to flick through – and they were willing to pay me a colossal £40 per hour to work on the project, from home, for 10 hours each week for several months. It was a godsend.

The magazine was also kick-started by the fact that I moved back to my parents' house for a few months, thereby saving on rent. My parents weren't impressed by my decision to leave my full-time job, and soon the atmosphere in the house became as frosty as it had been during my previous stay – although that doesn't mean I'm not grateful to my parents for letting me stay with them for free. The situation wasn't helped by the fact that my eldest sister, who had recently split from her husband, frequently came to the house in a distressed state. She was involved in a turbulent relationship with a new man. He was a combustible character, to put it mildly. He kept leaving her, coming back, and leaving again. At one point it seemed she'd had enough; she left him. Then she got pregnant by him. They were back together for a while. Then he left again. And so on. Living at home during this time was like living in an episode of EastEnders.

After a while, I became fed up not only of my home life, but of London life in general. Above all, I was getting sick of drunkenness. Londoners drink too much – whether it's in crowded expensive pubs where the punters stand cheek-to-jowl and nevertheless have to shout to be heard; or in dingy expensive nightclubs where the music is terrible and the bouncers are psychopaths; or at home, quaffing wine as though it's the epitome of sophistication and the only possible way to feel happy. I was also getting sick of people taking drugs. Good friends of mine – people I thought better of – would nip off to the toilet in the middle of a conversation to take some cocaine, then come back gurning like an excited farmer. I started to dread getting invited to social occasions just as much as I dreaded staying in while my parents polished off a bottle of wine in front of my volatile pregnant sister. It was time to roll the housing dice again.

5.

In the autumn of 2010, I moved back to Cambridge. I went back partly because I wanted to move out of my parents' house, partly because I was fed up of London, partly because the rent was (back then) slightly cheaper in Cambridge than in London, and partly because I still felt that I had unfinished business with Cambridge University. The idea of pursuing an academic career was gnawing at me. I figured that I could run *Cycle Lifestyle* from Cambridge. Most of my responsibilities didn't require me to be in London; I could make the fifty-mile trip every few weeks if necessary. In the meantime, I took on some philosophy tutoring again, and I became voluntary Co-ordinator of the University's Well-being Institute – a cross-disciplinary department that suited my desire to broaden my horizons as a philosopher.

The immediate catalyst for my move back to Cambridge was the availability of a room in a house belonging to the boyfriend of a female friend of mine. My friend had been one of my fellow PhD students in the History and Philosophy of Science Department where I studied; she had since moved away to take up an academic job in another city. Her boyfriend still lived in Cambridge, where he rented out the spare room in his house. With the nightmare of Kilburn fresh in my mind, I liked the idea of living with someone I already knew. I also liked the fact that the room was only going to cost me £354 per month.

My new landlord worked as an asset manager in a local financial firm. He was a nice guy. I don't think I could have put up with living with him for several years if he hadn't been. He was mostly considerate and generous. We used to enjoy hanging out together in the house from time to time. One of our favourite activities was watching sci-fi films or episodes of *Doctor Who* on TV. My landlord would cook up a delicious vegetable stew, which we'd eat with milkshakes followed by ice cream. Living with other people has its charms.

Unfortunately, it can also become cloying. My landlord's homely personality had a downside: he hardly ever left the house (except to go to work). Almost every evening, and usually throughout the weekends too, he would watch TV in the living room for hours on end. He was a film buff, and owned one of those luxurious giant flat-screen TVs, which he had hooked up to a powerful stereo system. I became accustomed to TV noises – Americans drawling, guns firing, sirens blazing, orchestras blaring, comedians wise-cracking, audiences laughing, adverts chirping, newsreaders intoning – seeping up through the floor in my bedroom. Amid this menagerie of sound, I couldn't write, because I couldn't think. Unless I was hanging out in the living room with my landlord, I usually spent my evenings in cafes.

Either that, or I was at 'proper' work. Once I had completed my consulting work for Brent Council, I needed to find some extra income, so I took on a job as a delivery driver for four nights each week at a local sushi restaurant in Cambridge. The job wasn't as depressing as it sounds – far from it. I really enjoy driving, and between deliveries I would sit and read a book, so the job was actually fuelling my creativity; you've got to fill your head with interesting ideas if you want interesting new ideas to come out of it. Gradually I settled into a pattern of focus and productivity, including writing the manuscript for *Einstein and the Art of Mindful Cycling*. With me at work most evenings, and my landlord at work most daytimes, our schedules dovetailed nicely. I mostly had the house to myself when he was at work, and vice versa.

But there was a complication. Ironically, one of the main sources of tension between me and my landlord was the very person who had put us in touch in the first place: my old friend. Over time, I'm sad to say, our friendship drifted into a sense of mutual unease. From her I learned my third lesson in surviving the housing crisis: beware of housemates' romantic partners. They don't pay rent, but you'll end up sharing the house – and therefore a large part of your life – with them.

My landlord's girlfriend was disruptive even when she wasn't in the house. She insisted on chatting to him at length on the phone immediately before she went to sleep every night. On a typical night, between around 10.30pm and midnight, I was treated to the sound of a one-way mobile phone conversation leaking out of my landlord's room as he lay in bed jabbering to his girlfriend. The sound of his deep voice penetrated ear plugs as well as walls, so I had no option but to grin and bear it. Getting to sleep was out of the question until the conversation was over. Worst of all, I couldn't concentrate on reading a book. I'm sure you know what it's like. You're trying to read something but – *so my colleague said he'd have to file the report as incomplete* – every few seconds you hear – *why don't you try getting it in green; it might look better* – someone else interrupting your – *I agree with your mum that your dad was wrong when he said that your sister had no right to say what she said* – thoughts. It's irritating. I became resentful of these late-night conversations. Previously, reading in bed had not only been one of the pleasures of my life, it had also helped me drift off to sleep. Now I was tossing and turning, staring at the ceiling, waiting for the babbling to end, whether in twenty minutes' time or an hours' time, the uncertainty compounding the irritation, and the irritation, in turn, taking its time to fade into the restfulness that precedes sleep. I asked my landlord if he could maybe chat to his girlfriend earlier in the evening. Nope, that was out of the question. I was powerless and frustrated.

And that was only the half of it. My landlord's girlfriend came to stay in the house frequently, usually for a week or so. Then, of course, I was subjected to a live, two-way babble from their bedroom every night. Moreover, when she was in residence I no longer had the house to myself during the daytimes. She would set up camp in the living area downstairs (an open plan lounge/kitchen), where she would work on various academic projects, often with the TV on in the background. Her academic specialism was the study of race. She was obsessed with race. They say that if your only tool is a hammer then everything looks like a nail; well, I guess if your only interest is race, then everything looks like racism. Everything, in other words, needs to be hammered into the shape of political correctness. My landlord's girlfriend was one of those people who see British culture as inherently racist, a culture chronically in need of remedial action in the form of relentless awareness-raising and affirmative action. Sitting in front of the TV in the evenings with my landlord, she used to provide live action commentary on each and every programme – from the news to the soap operas – during which she rancorously pointed out racist agendas, subtle or not so subtle, in almost everything anyone said or did.

Usually I let all this wash over me. But on one occasion, I didn't. I was watching football on TV one weekend when my landlord and his girlfriend arrived home from a shopping trip. His girlfriend took one look at the screen and said: "Eurgh."

"You don't like football?" I asked.

"It's racist," she replied. I should have known.

"In what way is football racist?" I asked, like a fish stupidly taking the bait.

"The fans are racist," she said.

"That's unfair," I explained. "There used to be a problem with some – *some* – racist football supporters in the 1970s and 80s, but that problem has been more or less eradicated from the game, certainly in Britain. There are ongoing campaigns to keep the game free of racism here – and rightly so."

"The commentators are racist," she continued; "they always describe non-white players as 'good specimens'."

"No they don't," I said. "Non-white players aren't necessarily valued for their athleticism. Far from it; many are considered highly creative and skilful. And plenty of white players are described as good specimens; for instance Cristiano Ronaldo, who is one of the best players in the world."

"Exactly, non-white players get less respect."

"Ooookay," I said, my exasperation rising to the surface like steam through the stratum of my self-control. "Pele, a black footballer from Brazil, is considered one of the greatest players – if not *the* greatest player – in the history of the game."

"Ah, but he wouldn't have thrived in England, would he?"

"Of course he would! I could give countless examples of successful black players in England. For instance, I'm a fan of Tottenham Hotspur, and the captain of our team is Ledley King – a black man from North London. He is an absolute gentleman, adored by all the fans, and a wonderful player. He is one of the most respected players in the history of the club."

At this point, my landlord chipped in, his girlfriend nodding approvingly: "He must have had to act white."

This whole conversation perfectly exemplified Theodore Dalrymple's dictum that 'there is no racist like an anti-racist'. As far as I can glean, my landlord and his girlfriend were arguing the following: if you're not white you're excluded from society, because as a non-white person you possess different characteristics to white people, and white people don't like your characteristics. By this logic, any non-white person who succeeds on the societal terms defined by white people must be a phoney and a sell-out. What a dismal and devious message! Anti-racist racists tell non-white people a grotesque and self-fulfilling lie while lamenting the divisive consequences of this lie.

"Who exactly is being racist?" I asked, as a miasma of mutual acrimony descended upon the room. I came to know that miasma well.

My landlord's relationship with his girlfriend was loving but tense. She was a devout Muslim from a devoutly Muslim family. Her parents were from Pakistan; they now lived in Birmingham, where she grew up. My landlord was a white Briton, and his girlfriend's family were wary of him. Even in her early thirties, she wasn't permitted to live with him as his partner. Occasionally her brothers would visit her while she was staying in Cambridge. They'd pull up in their big flashy cars, then sit in our lounge looking surly and suspicious. Sometimes – my landlord confided in me – members of his girlfriend's family called him a 'Kuffar', a highly derogatory Arabic term referring to non-Muslims.

Unsurprisingly, his girlfriend hated alcohol. Here, at least, there was common ground between her and I: while I was living London I had become increasingly disillusioned with Britain's drinking culture. But even on this common ground I elicited her disapproval. On one occasion, I was drinking an alcohol-free beer in the living room. I asked her if she wanted to taste it. "It's still beer; it's still forbidden," she insisted. Well, yes, it was beer, in the sense that an inflatable crocodile is a crocodile.

Pretend beer wasn't the only foodstuff that caused controversy in the house. My landlord was a meat eater, and so am I, but his girlfriend wasn't. She couldn't countenance the idea that the kitchen surfaces or implements had been in contact with meat – especially meat that wasn't halal – so we had a strict no meat policy in the house, whether she was in residence or not. I fell foul of this policy one evening, having accidentally cooked some pasta pouches that contained salami. It was a genuine mistake; I picked up the wrong packet in the supermarket. Alas, my landlord's girlfriend was in residence, and she spotted the empty packet on the kitchen worktop. I heard her frantically conferring with my landlord, who swiftly investigated. Frowning and shaking his head, he handed me a plastic fork and asked me to slide my meal off my plate and into a disposable tub. Then his girlfriend donned a pair of rubber gloves and proceeded to wash almost everything in the kitchen, as though she were some sort of chemical weapons decontamination expert. When I shambled in there to apologise she looked angrily up at me from the sink, her arms deep in suds, her face ashen. I promised it wouldn't happen again.

But it did, despite my best intentions. The next time, I was hanging out with a friend of mine. It was dinner time, and we decided to get pizzas from the supermarket. I confess that I didn't monitor which pizza my friend had chosen for himself. Naturally, I chose a vegetarian pizza, but my friend chose – you guessed it – ham and pineapple. This time my landlord raised the alarm, after spotting the empty pizza box in the recycling bin.

"Um – is this a meat pizza?" he enquired, as a look of dismay crossed his face, a look of horror crossed his girlfriend's face, a look of weary realisation crossed my face, and a look of confusion crossed my friend's face.

"Oh dear, I'm sorry," I said, swiftly opening the oven door and waving away the steam. My friend had only just put the pizza into the oven; perhaps disaster could be averted. I put the pizza straight back in its box and tried to offer some words of consolation to my landlord's girlfriend.

"I'm really sorry. Don't worry, the ham hasn't touched anything. It hasn't touched any pans or surfaces. It hasn't touched the inside of the oven. It was just sitting there on top of the pizza. You don't need to do your OCD ritual like last time."

As you can probably tell, words of consolation aren't my forte. A few minutes later, I went back into the kitchen, where I found my landlord and his girlfriend once again in frantic conversation. My landlord looked up and announced: "We are both offended by what you just said."

"The OCD ritual?" I asked.

He nodded.

I decided to come out fighting.

"You've no right to be offended," I asserted. "I'm sorry for breaking the house rule, but I'm not sorry for my interpretation of what happened last time. I don't believe in religious rites. I don't believe in God. That's why I believe that washing the entire kitchen is unnecessary – a form of neurosis, an obsessive ritual. My interpretation is no less credible than yours."

And with that, a permanent miasma descended.

6.

Over time, I found that being in the presence of my landlord's girlfriend had a profoundly demoralising effect on me. Her views on race were the tip of the iceberg of her deep-seated, religiously-motivated antipathy to Western values in general. She saw our freedoms as a recipe for self-indulgence, our democracy as a recipe for manipulation, our secularism as a recipe for immorality, our science as a recipe for depredation, our international trade as a recipe for exploitation, and our capitalistic economic system as a recipe for greed. She saw all these vices as manifested in endemic racism, especially racism against people who challenge the mainstream, especially racism against Muslims (this last part being particularly absurd: Islam is not a race; in fact, Islam is the most ethnically diverse religion in Britain). She saw her fellow citizens as the brainwashed executors of Western imperialism. What she didn't see was the irony in all this: that she herself had been elevated by the UK's education system to an influential position where she was permitted – even encouraged – to mercilessly castigate the West. Her views were self-undermining.

Yet they were unshakeable. Her dismal attitude to life was partly the result of her religious beliefs, and partly the result of her belief in socialism. Either way, she saw herself and her (likeminded) academic colleagues as playing a crucial role in creating a better world. The more that intellectuals such as her could convince people to reject the racist capitalist mainstream, the more that intellectuals such as her would receive support from the public, and the more that intellectuals such as her would be empowered to reshape society according to their own supposedly more enlightened goals and methods. Of course, as a Muslim my landlord's girlfriend didn't always agree with other socialists about how exactly society should be reshaped. Nonetheless, all anti-capitalists agree on the most important thing, the thing that defines them: capitalism is the enemy.

I can't deny that I felt personally affronted by these views. I had left academic philosophy partly because I wanted to embrace real life – to embrace the reality of the world and of my own freedom, and to embrace all the economic and political opportunities that were available to me. I had founded my cycling magazine business because I wanted to make some money while supporting a good cause. I was working extremely hard for little financial reward. Yet here I was repeatedly being told that I was part of the problem, not part of the solution. In other words: I had left academic philosophy because I was fed up of witnessing intellectuals benefitting from making a problem out of real life and its opportunities. The last thing I wanted was to re-enter that miasma of lazy cynicism when I walked into my own living room.

My sense of chronic irritation wasn't helped by the fact that my landlord eagerly agreed with his girlfriend about most things, especially socialism. Having completed a Master's degree in 'Postmodernism' a few years previously, he was a fully paid-up supporter of the idea that society takes primacy over individuals. He was, indeed, an evangelist for this idea. People who call themselves postmodernists believe that nothing exists apart from society. They believe that there are no real individuals and there is no real world; all that exists is a sort of social ether. This social ether, so it goes, constitutes itself through its ideas – ideas expressed in words and images and signs and symbols – and in doing so it literally creates its individual members and the world beyond. In this way, postmodernism lends itself to the most extreme form of socialism. Postmodernists believe that to overcome capitalism, 'we' as a society simply need to reimagine ourselves as a harmonious collective and, in the process, reimagine reality, for the benefit of all. My landlord's girlfriend agreed with him about all this, her only caveat being that as a society we should reinvent ourselves along Islamic lines because God, supposedly, is real – that is, *really real*, not just a creation of society – and, accordingly, God's commandments have priority over our own.

Obviously, my landlord's belief in an extreme version of socialism was hard to reconcile with the fact that he was an asset manager in a financial firm. I suppose he was forlornly waiting for 'society' to abolish banks so he could live happily ever after. In the meantime, he laboured under the weight of an intense ambivalence towards his work. On one hand, he wanted to earn enough money to buy lots of film DVDs and TV boxsets that he could spend his non-working hours watching in the comfort of his own home. On the other hand, he wanted the veil of capitalism to be lifted from his eyes, whereupon the pristine landscape of a socialist utopia would be revealed to him. He coped with this ambivalence by promising himself that one fine day in the future he would resign as an asset manager and become a writer. Occasionally, he spent his spare time trying to write a book about postmodernism – a fiction book, appropriately enough – and this pastime became a sort of barometer for his mood. If I came home and found him hunched over his laptop instead of watching TV, I knew he had had a bad day at the office.

Either that, or he had had an argument with his girlfriend. She didn't like him writing. Not one bit. She wanted him to have a good wage, a good career, a good car, a good house – nothing more, nothing less. Obviously, there's nothing wrong with these things *per se*. But my landlord didn't want them *per se*. As barmy as his postmodernist ideas were, he wanted to be creative. Indeed, I suspect that his belief in postmodernism would have evaporated once he had escaped from the career he resented; he would have no further need for political fantasies once he started living the creative life he really wanted to live. One weekend, he announced to me that he had made up his mind: he was going part-time in his job, so he could focus on writing his book. Alas, his resolve lasted about three hours, before his girlfriend drove a stake through it during their late-evening phone session. Here was a dedicated opponent of the West, a dedicated opponent of capitalism, a dedicated opponent of a system she saw as imperialist and racist, insisting that her partner continued working full time in a bank, mining capitalism to full effect, so she could continue to enjoy the lifestyle to which she was accustomed.

You can draw your own conclusions. My landlord ultimately drew his: he converted to Islam a few years ago.

7.

As an adult, I've never been religious, but I was a socialist for many years, starting in my teens and continuing into my early thirties. Around the time I was living with my landlord and his girlfriend, my socialist beliefs started to evaporate. There were various reasons for this – each reason reinforcing the other.

First and foremost, there was my own personal experience of working on *Cycle Lifestyle*. Through running a business I came to realise that my fellow socialists had misled me about capitalism. Although capitalism isn't a perfect system (and I've written at length about its imperfections in the *Journal of Modern Wisdom*), socialists tend to caricaturise the commercial sector to the point of misrepresenting it. The commercial sector isn't full of rapacious, nasty, selfish, greedy, heartless slave-drivers. Most business-people are characteristically polite, helpful, conscientious, empathetic, hardworking and fair. Most businesspeople are almost obsessively eager to find ways in which they can work with other people – whether their employees and colleagues, or strangers – towards mutual gain.

I also came to realise that the bogey word used by the left – 'competitive' – is a superficial way of summing up the commercial sector. Insofar as businesses compete with each other to make money, the main driver of success in this competition is *cooperation*. To succeed, businesses must cooperate with each other while also fostering cooperation amongst their own employees. Capitalism could be defined as the economic system in which people compete to be the most cooperative. A more virtuous system could hardly be imagined. Nor indeed could a more 'inclusive' system. After all, money doesn't discriminate; hence capitalism is a powerful antidote to discrimination. Any business that shuns opportunities for cooperation with so-called marginalised groups – such as women, disabled people, religious or ethnic minorities, homosexuals, or anyone else – will be at a competitive disadvantage compared to a business that embraces as many opportunities as possible. Competitive cooperation systematically drives out prejudice.

In turn, I came to realise that the word 'profit' likewise doesn't deserve its negative reputation among socialists. Yes, there are a few unscrupulous businesspeople around. Yes, there are a few profiteers, especially among the biggest, most powerful corporations. But, on the whole, making a profit simply means deriving an advantage from fulfilling other people's needs and freely chosen desires. In other words, a profit is a reward for helpful behaviour, and a big profit is a reward for very helpful behaviour. What's not to like?

Alongside my personal experience of working in the commercial sector, I also learned a lot from reading books by conservative intellectuals, such as Matt Ridley, Roger Scruton, James Bartholomew,

James Delingpole and Theodore Dalrymple, as well as books by Steven Pinker, who I suppose could be described as a pro-capitalism centrist. From all these authors I learned that capitalism has proven itself throughout history to be *by far* the best economic system. Capitalism fosters wealth, innovation, technological development, trust, democracy, and peace. Indeed, all these forms of progress have never been more evident than they are today, with democratic capitalism having spread rapidly throughout the world, creating an unprecedentedly peaceful and productive era, and – in the last two decades alone – lifting a billion people out of extreme poverty.

In contrast – I also learned – socialism fails miserably where capitalism succeeds. When governments try to control the economy, they invariably fail to replicate the spectacular results that the free market achieves. No government is capable of judging who needs what and when and how as efficiently and effectively as free people can. Employees of the state – no matter how enlightened and determined they supposedly are – are above all incentivised to respond to the dictates of their political paymasters, not to the real needs of the population. Over time, governments tend to create huge stultifying bureaucratic structures – as in, for instance, the UK's state education system or National Health Service, both of which, note, socialists themselves are always complaining about.

I came to realise that socialists are accustomed to blaming capitalism and businesses for the failings of socialism. Over the last half century, government spending in the UK has risen persistently in real terms, including under so-called conservative administrations. Yet during this period socialists have become increasingly angry and vociferous; they have relentlessly demanded tax increases and more government spending, particularly in the areas – education and health – where escalating government spending has failed so conspicuously. In contrast, no one ever complains that we need more government spending on mobile phone technology. Here, the commercial sector has made stupendous advances, to the point where the poorest people today can easily afford technological wizardry that just a few decades ago was out of reach of the richest people.

Even where socialism is apparently most defensible – namely, in its demand for generous state welfare provision – the landscape is strewn with failure. By allocating welfare support on the basis of 'need', socialism encourages applicants to enter into an arms race of irresponsibility and misbehaviour. The more one screws up one's life – not to mention the lives of one's dependents and neighbours – the more one 'needs' welfare. Hence, the enormous expansion of Britain's welfare bureaucracy over the last 70 years has ushered in an era of pandemic social problems, including family breakdown, alcoholism, drug abuse, mental illness, crime, teenage pregnancy, and educational failure. Added to these disasters is the widespread problem of benefit fraud, a problem which mushroomed under the last Labour administration. Of course, some claimants of state benefits are deserving. But that is the whole point. The welfare state is adept at diverting funds away from people who deserve to be helped.

By catalysing irresponsibility, by squashing the economic productivity that brings material progress to the masses, and by sidelining deserving welfare claimants, socialism doesn't cure poverty, it exacerbates poverty. In the process, socialism makes a travesty of its own claim to be an egalitarian system; socialism weighs on the poor disproportionately, while the rich disappear further into the economic distance. Moreover, by entrenching state power, socialism ultimately creates a class of government monopolists who are more powerful and more corrupt, and hence more destructive of the common good, than any plutocrat could ever be. When socialism is unopposed, it ends in corruption, oppression, starvation, environmental depredation, strife and bloodshed, every time – such is the lesson of socialism in the twentieth century, whether in the form of communism or National Socialism. Compared to the swamp created by the failings of socialism in practice, capitalism has created a Garden of Eden. And note: *that is the relevant comparison*. There is no point comparing the proven results of capitalism – imperfect though they may be – to a fanciful socialist utopia that doesn't and cannot exist.

In the end, the only thing socialism reliably achieves is to make socialists better off. Socialists, I came to realise, are philosophical hypochondriacs with a political streak. By convincing people that capitalism is a problem that only socialism can solve, socialists are able to hang back from life while claiming the moral high ground. Alas, in doing so, socialists also succeed in distracting and discouraging themselves and their fellow citizens from doing what *can* be done to genuinely improve society. Liberalisation – including the liberalisation of healthcare and education, with all the benefits of competitive cooperation this would entail – is just the start of what can be done.

People who are on the margins of society can be cajoled into the mainstream – into employment and, more generally, into a life of responsibility and productivity – rather than being trapped on welfare, or, worse, being told that capitalism is evil because it has supposedly discriminated against them. Meanwhile, welfare can be provided less corruptibly and more impactfully by a variety of means other than state subventions, whether by families, communities, charities or insurance schemes (the kinds of insurance schemes, incidentally, which fund healthcare in almost all other civilised countries).

But here's the rub: these human-level solutions to human social problems require people to display genuine cooperation, to genuinely support each other, to participate in genuine communities, or to make a genuine contribution to a collective enterprise. For socialists it is far easier, and, in many cases, more remunerative, to sit back and moan about capitalism than to work towards a better society. Indeed, a better society is the last thing socialists want: it would deprive them of their role and their privileges, whether these privileges take the form of a government salary, or just a superior reputation.

The more I learned about both capitalism and socialism, the keener I was to discuss with my fellow socialists the new ideas I was encountering. My political affiliation, after all, didn't change overnight. In the interests of accuracy and balance, I felt I had a responsibility to highlight the benefits of capitalism, and the flaws of socialism, to people whom I saw as my allies. At the very least, I assumed that socialists would furnish me with the relevant counter-arguments if it turned out I had been misled by the right-wingers.

However, I was surprised by the way that socialists reacted to my new perspective. I wasn't surprised that they didn't agree with what I was saying. I was surprised that they didn't exactly disagree with me either – at least, not in the sense of providing counter-arguments or disputing the factual correctness of what I was saying. Socialists simply refused to engage with any of the points I was making. I might as well have been talking to a brick wall. A brick wall daubed with a load of slogans.

For instance, if I said that capitalism fosters mutual gain from the top to the bottom of the economic scale, socialists would say "the workers are enslaved". If I said that money enables strangers to work together on complex projects, socialists would say "chasing profits is greedy". If I said that unemployment has risen under every Labour government in UK history, socialists would say "Margaret Thatcher closed the mines". If I said that capitalism promotes racial and social har-mony because money doesn't discriminate, socialists would say "white males are privileged". If I said that competitive cooperation provides a much stronger incentive for hard work than the collectivisation of rewards, socialists would say "capitalism causes in-equality". If I said that inequality can be a *motivation*, not a hindrance, to poorer people, socialists would say they want to live in a "decent society" or a "caring society". If I said that inequality is also curtailed by the fact that rich businesses can be pegged back by competitors cutting prices, socialists would say "the economy should be planned". If I said that government regulations usually favour big businesses at the expense of small businesses, socialists would say "deregulation caused the banking crisis". If I said that the banking crisis was partly caused by people borrowing irresponsibly, socialists would say "we are all responsible for each other". If I said that there are other ways to display social solidarity than through socialism, socialists would say "it's the government's job to help the poor". If I said that the welfare state can sometimes trap people in poverty, socialists would say "austerity is evil". If I said that balancing the books in government is no bad thing, socialists would say "raise taxes, or borrow more". And, in the end, if I said that there is a limit, any limit, to what government spending can achieve, socialists would shake their heads and say "Tories are selfish".

I soon found that this idea that conservatives are selfish – or, worse, "nasty", "scum", "vermin", "evil", etc. – was a sort of black hole into which every discussion with a socialist descended. The more my fellow socialists evaded the points I was making, the more I would double down on reason, painstakingly supplying more arguments and more evidence, in the naïve hope that this was what socialists needed, as though I were performing some sort of public service. In fact, by doubling down on reason I was merely serving to accelerate the conversation towards its inevitable conclusion – that anyone who disagrees with socialism is a heartless bastard. My fellow socialists, I soon realised, were not interested in reality, at least not in the context of politics. Reality had the potential to make them question whether they were a good person or not. Socialists don't always agree with postmodernists that reality doesn't exist, but all socialists are swift to sacrifice realism on the altar of their self-regard. And, as a result, socialists are swift to shun *people* who champion realism in politics;

Tories are branded as callous, so as to atone for the socialists' own callousness.

This scapegoating dynamic has one feature which I found most dastardly of all. Naturally, if you attempt to reason with someone who offers only slogans and epithets, you are likely to feel quite frustrated; the Buddha himself would be exasperated by someone who kept banging on about Thatcher closing the mines. However, when a critic of socialism displays any signs of exasperation whatsoever – perhaps by sighing or puffing out their cheeks or rolling their eyes, never mind raising their voice or offering a rebuke – socialists take this as an indication of the malignity of capitalism. Anyone who responds angrily to the idea of an egalitarian paradise, so it goes, must be a right bastard (pun intended). Consequently, when you find yourself in a frustrating conversation with a socialist, you soon get the impression that you are only succeeding in reminding them what *not* to believe – namely, *whatever you are saying* – because whatever you are saying must be wrong if you are saying it exasperatedly. A crushing sense of futility is your reward for starting out with a good attitude.

Above all, it was my fellow socialists who pushed me away from socialism. I was pushed away by numerous frustrating experiences of trying and failing to have a rational conversation with socialists about society. When I was running *Cycle Lifestyle*, I used to get invited to a lot of events organised by lefty types, whether 'Cycling Officers' or 'Environment Officers' in local authorities or universities. Almost every time, I ended up departing with a sense of unwarranted shame, clambouring wearily out of a black hole of opprobrium after I had stupidly taken the bait when someone declared themselves to be an opponent of capitalism.

Against this backdrop – a backdrop of me campaigning on all fronts – the atmosphere of pious anti-capitalism in my own house started to bother me even more. I wanted – no I *needed* – to come home to a sanctuary, not to an antechamber of further censure. I needed to think things over, to reflect, to consolidate, not to listen to my landlord and his girlfriend heckling the TV, forever interjecting about how disgusting and racist and decadent the West supposedly is, while they personally couldn't be bothered to do anything about it other than sit on the sofa complaining and eating. Indeed, I didn't want to hear the TV either. And, when the TV was finally switched off, I didn't want to lie awake in bed at night waiting for two people who didn't think that reality existed to stop filling my real bedroom with real noise.

8.

In short, I was desperate to move out. In early 2013, I started looking for an alternative place to live in Cambridge. I couldn't afford a house of my own in town, so I kept an eye out for shared houses that looked tolerable. But every time I checked out a room, there was always an aspect of the arrangement that set alarm bells ringing in my head. For instance, there'd be someone in the house who got up for work at 4am. Or someone who played the trombone. Or someone who smoked dope. Or there'd be... well, people I didn't know, who could have any number of annoying habits. I was even put off by friendly people. Maybe they'd turn out to be 'sociable' – eek! My years of dysfunctional shared living had made me hypersensitive about sharing a house with anyone. I was pining for my own space.

One day, an online advert caught my eye. It was for a single-occupancy 'annex' in a village in the countryside 10 miles east of Cambridge. I knew the area well, because I often went on long bike rides out into the Fens – the perfectly flat agricultural expanse that extends from Cambridge into East Anglia and all the way to the North Sea. The prospect of living in the Fens appealed to me, because it's incredibly quiet and calm out there. It would certainly give me the space I craved. And I was enthused by the idea that I could rent the annex and live completely on my own, undisturbed, for a modest £600 a month.

So I rode out on my bike to take a look, and I was smitten, right away. The annex, despite its name, was detached from the main property, which was owned by two doctors – a married couple – and their children. The only adjoining building was a massive garden shed, but there wouldn't be any disturbance from there. The whole structure was built into the slope of an old quarry, down which ivy and other climbing plants tumbled in a profusion of green. One of my friends later remarked that the annex looked like a hobbit house. That suited me just fine. I immediately agreed to move in. And so it was that I found myself living in the idyllic village of Swaffham Prior.

Unfortunately, things got off to a less-than-ideal start. The doctors had two teenage daughters, one of whom owned a horse that needed to be fed every morning. On weekdays, she got up early to do it before she went to college. The horse was kept in a field a few miles away – too far to walk, so the daughter rode a moped over there. Hence, five days a week, at 6am, I was woken by the sound of a moped engine revving explosively up the driveway beneath my window. I had to admire the daughter's dedication. But I couldn't believe my bad luck. I had come all this way, into the middle of nowhere, only to be confounded by noise again. Nothing blocked out the sound. I tried boarding up my bedroom window with wood, and draping bed sheets down the insides of the walls, to no avail. The problem was exacerbated by the fact that I was working on deliveries most evenings in Cambridge, so I wasn't arriving home until midnight. And, in the mornings, after the moped had woken me, sometimes I couldn't doze off again. The ensuing lack of sleep was a disaster for my creative output. Without seven or eight hours sleep, I couldn't crank my bleary mind into the realm of abstract thought where, for me, philo-sophical ideas happen.

This frustrating situation went on for a few months. Eventually I decided I would have to move out. Then, suddenly, the noise stopped. No more early-morning moped. A mystery! Later that week, I bumped into the male doctor outside the main house. He said he had some sad news: the horse had died. I hope you won't think I'm a bad person when I tell you that I had mixed feelings about this tragedy.

I soon settled into a peaceful and happy life in the annex. I started work on an essay about socialism; this essay would ultimately grow into my second book, *Scapegoated Capitalism*. In the meantime, I was also busy with my evening job. I was working for a curry takeaway business which was owned by a married couple – an English lady of Indian descent and her East Anglian husband. Like me, they had recently moved to Cambridge from London. I got on well with both of them; they were hardworking and intelligent, and we used to enjoy discussing business together. I convinced them to let me do most of my deliveries on an electric bicycle. In the congested, narrow streets of Cambridge I could usually reach the customers much quicker by e-bike than by car. And – as a felicitous side-effect – I got much fitter.

I acquired the electric bike in exchange for an advert in *Cycle Lifestyle*. At this stage, I was still running the magazine. Indeed, it had just had its most successful year. Things were looking up in my life, in all but one respect: I didn't have enough money. The extra rent, combined with the fuel costs of getting to and from town, meant that my bank balance was gradually sinking into the red. The old dilemma raised its head again: if I wanted to live in a suitable house such as this, I would have to find a better-paid job.

An obvious option was for me to become a teacher. I didn't have a teaching qualification, but with my degree I was eligible to work as a cover teacher, for which I could earn around £100 a day. Cover teaching appealed to me, because I would only have to turn up in the morning, teach a few random lessons, then go home at the end of the school day. I wouldn't have to fulfil the wider responsibilities of being a proper teacher – for instance, marking the kids' work, planning lessons, writing reports, dealing with parents, and filling out hundreds of forms. So I registered with a teaching agency, and soon I was spending my days covering a variety of lessons in a variety of secondary schools in Cambridgeshire.

I enjoyed this experience, and I learned a lot from it. But – in keeping with the old dilemma – cover teaching massively undermined my creativity. For one thing, the job was exhausting, both physically and mentally; in both senses, you have to stay on your toes as a teacher, all day long. Moreover, as an agency cover teacher, keeping discipline is especially challenging. The kids think they can push the boundaries when you're an anonymous outsider. That's not to say I had problems keeping order in class; I didn't. For me, the problem was that when I got home at 4pm, I was absolutely shattered from the day's exertions. There was no chance of me working on my writing in the evenings.

Financially I didn't need to work as a cover teacher every day. But unfortunately I couldn't create a block of free days by stipulating when I wanted to teach. The way the system operates is that you have to keep your phone switched on early each morning and wait for a call from the agency. Sometimes the call comes; sometimes it doesn't. To ensure I had enough work, I needed to be available five days a week. As a result, my routine was disrupted not just on the days when I was offered work, but on the days when I wasn't. Each morning I had to be up early and ready, dressed in my suit and tie, waiting for a call. If the call didn't come, I sometimes found it hard to segue into my writing, either because I was tired, or because I was in the wrong frame of mind: working on a big writing project is much more difficult without continuity.

After a few months of working as a cover teacher for the agency, I was offered a full-time job at a nice secondary school just down the road from my house. I decided to take the job, because I figured that if I wasn't getting much writing done I might as well be earning an income five days a week. At Bottisham Village College, I was a sort of odd-job teacher, with a variety of teaching roles including plenty of cover teaching but also some temporary roles as a proper teacher (Bottisham is an 'Academy' school, which means it is permitted to employ so-called 'unqualified' teachers). This set-up lasted for about a year, at which point the old dilemma interjected again: I was desperate to get on with some writing. I decided to make yet another attempt to achieve a balance between earning enough money and living a creative life. My idea was to cut my commitment at Bottisham to three days a week, and on the other four evenings work as a delivery driver. This arrangement would give me four consecutive mornings on which I could write without interruption. Hence, in early 2014 I went back to my previous driving job – part-time – at the Indian takeaway, and I started grinding out the chapters of *Scapegoated Capitalism*.

Meanwhile, I was also trying to keep *Cycle Lifestyle* going. But its days were numbered. I was struggling to attract any investment at all. In the fifth and final year I made just a few hundred pounds in profit; I was basically working for free. And that wasn't the only reason I was struggling to motivate myself to work on the magazine. Collaborating with the local authorities was proving a nightmare, not least because they were slow to reply to my correspondence, and even slower to make a decision; no one seemed to be able to take responsibility for anything. Objectively speaking, I was offering them a great deal. For a bargain price I would produce thousands of bespoke local copies of a high-quality magazine and deliver them to any number of venues. However, as ever, actual results and value for money didn't matter to the bureaucrats. They were more concerned about the overall impression the magazine would make with their colleagues and superiors – an impression which, in its nebulousness, took time to ascertain. One local authority, after a long period of correspondence, declined to work with me because *the magazine was made of paper* – this apparently wasn't considered environmentally friendly. When I reassured them that the magazine was printed on Forest Stewardship Council-approved stocks, I was told: "We're concerned about the image we're projecting." Image was everything: I was wasting my time bringing reality into it.

Sometimes I felt I was dealing with a bunch of adolescents, such was the lack of professionalism in the local authorities. On one occasion when I hadn't heard back from a cycling officer whom I had been corresponding with, I chased him up, whereupon he sent me a long rambling reply telling me that he was having a fraught relationship with his lover, and this was having an impact on his work, and blah, blah, blah. Maybe this sort of melodrama went down well with his colleagues; maybe it got him off the hook whenever he failed to fulfil his meagre duties. As for me, I was tempted to send a reply saying: "why are telling me this?" But I replied politely, of course. I wanted to work with him, because I wanted to earn money. Don't let anyone ever tell you that capitalism isn't a force for tolerance, patience, good will and constructive behaviour.

Prior to this, I had also had a lot of trouble working with a man called Simon Parker. A kind of Harry Beck figure for cycle routes, Parker is the originator of the 'London Cycle Map' for which my magazine was campaigning. In 2011, the London Cycle Map Campaign had reached the finals of Ordinance Survey's 'Geovation' competition – a national competition which was set up to highlight the latest 'transport innovations' in the UK. Ironically, my serious problems with Parker began when we won the competition. After the final, I magnanimously (some would say stupidly) allowed Parker to collect the £12,000 prize money, even though my assistant editor and I had done almost all the work during the arduous competition process. Parker and I agreed to share the money 50/50, and shook hands on it. But he reneged on the deal; he released only a fraction of the funds. The judges had awarded us the prize money on the basis that I would organise a conference to which officials from every London borough would be invited, to discuss plans for a city-wide network of signed and colour-coded cycle routes (such a conference was, I figured, the only way to get responsibility-averse government officials to take the London Cycle Map seriously). However, without sufficient funds, the conference never happened – a great loss, not just for me but for London.

Parker was behaving extremely erratically around this time. For years he had lived like a hobo, working occasionally, squatting in the capital, and attending raves; it was a lifestyle that meant he often needed quick cash. He started phoning up the campaign's long-term sponsors – who were one of my most important advertising customers – and asking them for money. He even visited their office and begged for some cash, which they gave him. He had no right, and they had no obligation: my business relationship with Parker was solely a cross-publicity agreement, as per a contract we had signed; the arrangements I had with my advertisers were nothing to do with him, as he well knew. Alas, the sponsors of the campaign terminated their involvement with my magazine as soon as they realised that Parker was acting improperly. I lost thousands of pounds as a result, and the whole experience was utterly demoralising.

Added to all this, by the time I was living in Swaffham Prior I simply didn't have the time or money to travel to London regularly enough to make a success of the magazine. In particular, my teaching job was getting in the way. On one occasion, I was invited onto BBC breakfast TV to discuss cycling, but I had to decline because I had to be in school. I was over-worked – working seven days a week, as well as trying to research and write a book. I started suffering from insomnia. Some nights I was so stressed I didn't sleep at all – not a wink. On one such occasion, by 7am I decided something had to give. I had been mulling over the idea of closing down *Cycle Lifestyle* for a long time, and now I knew it was time. I went downstairs and made myself a super-strong coffee, then I sat at my computer. I proceeded to spend the day reconfiguring the magazine's website. I didn't want the London Cycle Map Campaign to have been in vain, so I converted the website into a showcase for the campaign. Then I sent out an email notifying my customers and colleagues that the magazine was closing. Then, I must confess, I burst into tears.

This was a sad period in my life. I felt like a failure. I had set out to become a writer, but I had little to show for it other than one published book and an ex-business that had not only failed to make me enough money to live on but had also failed to give me much free time to work on my writing. My grand plan to pursue a creative life had culminated in me living like an exile in the middle of nowhere, working seven days a week at two jobs, and still struggling to pay the rent. My disillusionment was compounded by the fact that I had made hardly any progress with my most cherished goal: finding a publisher who would work with me on a book about philosophical hypochondria. I wanted to write about how philosophers and other intellectuals hide from life by hiding behind dismal theories and ideologies. But, ironically, I could hardly find anyone in publishing, whether in academic or commercial publishing, who wasn't a philosophical hypochondriac and therefore intensely averse to my proposals. I did manage to work with several top agents, and on separate occasions I managed to convince commissioning editors at Penguin and Profile Books to publish a book about philosophical hypochondria. But on both occasions, their colleagues subsequently vetoed the project. There are some things, apparently, you can't say in print.

Soon after I had given up on *Cycle Lifestyle*, I reacted to my sense of failure by intensifying my efforts to succeed as a writer. Working as a teacher, even for three days a week, was hurting my creativity, so I knew I had to leave Bottisham Village College. However, leaving was very hard. I had become good friends with many of my fellow teachers, having discovered the general truth that teachers are some of the best people you're ever likely to meet, regardless of their politics. I was also enjoying interacting with the pupils at Bottisham, who were generally well behaved and fun to be around. But I had to leave.

In the summer of 2014, I quit teaching and started working six nights a week at my delivery job in Cambridge. I redoubled my efforts on *Scapegoated Capitalism*, and I battened down the hatches financially. But again, inexorably, I started sliding into the red. This time, however, I had no appetite for taking refuge in another well-paid job. Instead, I found refuge in an unexpected place.

9.

The idea of moving out of the annex entered my head not long after I quit teaching. The truth is, I was lonely in Swaffham Prior. There was no evening bus service between the village and Cambridge, so I hardly ever had visitors, apart from the enormous hairy spiders that wandered in from the shed on a daily basis, and the squirrels that cavorted in the rafters at night (or, rather, I *hoped* they were squirrels, not rats). In the mornings I found myself eating breakfast alone, then staring at my computer screen, and feeling an overwhelming urge to talk to someone, anyone, face to face. The village had no shops or cafes, so I couldn't pop out for a quick social interaction. Often I would drive into Cambridge where I would remain all day before going to my delivery job in the evening. I realised I could improve my mood and save a lot of money by moving back into town.

Of course, there was still the problem of the prohibitive cost of renting a whole flat or house in Cambridge. I was lonely, yes, but I wasn't lonely enough to want to move back into a shared house. Suddenly, however, an unlikely solution presented itself. I stumbled across an advert for a single-occupancy dwelling that was described as a 'summer room'. It was located in Romsey, the same suburb I had previously lived in with my landlord and his girlfriend. I loved Romsey, and I was intrigued by the idea of a 'summer room', especially since the room was available for an inexplicably low rent of £450 a month.

When I went to take a look, I found out why the summer room was so cheap. It was a small building at the bottom of someone's garden. There was no kitchen or bathroom in the room, but it had an electric heater and a microwave, and was quite modern and smart, having been constructed just a few years previously. Occupants of the room were given a key to a side door of the main house, so they could access the kitchen and a downstairs bathroom. All in all, it seemed a pretty good deal. I rarely cooked dinner at home because I was eating a free curry almost every night at work. And the idea of walking 20 yards to the main house to use the bathroom didn't deter me. As a student at Cambridge, I had lived in an historic court in a room located more than 20 yards from the bathroom. I'd had to walk through an open-air corridor and down a flight of steps to go to the toilet, and this didn't bother me; in fact, I found the whole experience romantic and inspiring. Likewise, I figured, living in the summer room would be fun in its own way – like a permanent camping trip. Above all, it would give me my own space.

The only deterrent was that the owner of the property, who lived in the main house, seemed a bit of a weirdo. When I first went to look at the summer room he insisted on taking me on an hour-long tour of the whole premises. Before entering the main house, he asked me to don a pair of plastic slippers. He proceeded to show me how to operate almost every household appliance, with an attention to detail that seemed excessive, especially given that I hadn't yet agreed to move in; there was an optimum way to flush the toilet, a strict procedure for using the washing machine, even a specific method for filling and pouring the kettle. Almost every aspect of life in the house was covered by rules. Some of these rules were normal – such as don't leave a mess in the kitchen; don't leave hairs in the shower; don't dry wet clothes without opening the window. Others were a bit odder – such as don't put anything the bin without tying each item of rubbish into the smallest possible knot; don't own more than one box of breakfast cereal; don't put clothes on the washing line without using exactly the correct number of pegs per item; don't leave any – *any* – drops of water on the kitchen surfaces or floor. Clearly, this man had an extreme case of OCD (either that, or he was obeying an unusually pedantic deity).

Still, I figured that I wouldn't be hassled too much while I was living down in the summer room. I agreed to move in, and I signed an exquisitely detailed contract. All the rules, I soon discovered, were policed with fanatical diligence by my landlord. Sometimes he would come down to the summer room and rap on my door to inform me that I had broken a house rule. There was no point in disputing the veracity of his claims, or indeed the validity of his rules: he wouldn't go away until I had apologised and agreed not to break the rule again. But generally, my hunch was correct: as long as I conducted myself impeccably in the main house, I enjoyed an undisturbed existence in my garden retreat.

For about six months, a period that included the winter of 2014/15, I lived happily in the summer room.

I had everything I needed there as a writer: a desk, a bed, a sofa, a bookshelf, warmth, and peace and quiet. The only sound that ever woke me was the chirruping of birds. Even my mum, when she visited, approved of my new home – the ultimate seal of approval, one might say. Admittedly, I had made some sacrifices in moving out of the annex in Swaffham Prior. I had owned too many possessions to fit them all in the summer room, so I had given most of my stuff away to charity shops. In the process, I culled about two thirds of my books, a collection I had enthusiastically acquired since my undergraduate days. Giving up these books, I felt I was losing part of myself, part of my history. But I gained something better: a life unencumbered, in more ways than one. With my six-nights-a-week delivery job making me enough money to live off, with my magazine business wrapped up, and with no housemates bothering me with their antics or their politics, for the first time since completing my PhD I possessed what I craved: the physical and mental space to write every day. I made the most of it.

10.

If things had turned out differently, I might still be living in the summer room. I might never have written this book about housing, because my own personal housing crisis might have petered out before it became something of an obsession for me.

Alas, I soon discovered that not everyone approved of my new home. One day, there was a knock on my door. I opened it, and initially I was unsurprised: it was my landlord, standing outside with a grave expression on his face. What was it this time? Drops of water? Hairs? Too many pegs? Unknotted rubbish? No, this time it was something else. He had received a letter from the City Council warning him that he was in contravention of the law. Renting out the summer room was illegal, and a housing inspector was coming to view the room in few days to confirm as much. If I didn't move out immediately, my landlord could be fined or possibly jailed.

What could the reason be? What was wrong with the summer room? Did it come with some fault or danger that my eagled-eyed worrier of a mum hadn't spotted? Nope. But it was illegal nonetheless. There is a law in Britain against letting out so-called 'Beds in Sheds'. These are defined as dwellings that don't have a bathroom and a kitchen and aren't directly connected to a main property that does. The government considers Beds in Sheds 'substandard'. The typical examples are garden sheds or garages, converted into basic living quarters by so-called 'rogue' landlords who are seeking to meet a rampant demand for affordable housing. My summer room was unusual in that it was purpose-built; I'm sure it was of a higher standard than most Beds in Sheds. Even so, I wasn't allowed to live there.

I'm not sure who tipped off the Council. It was probably a neighbour. Or possibly it was some builders who had recently done some work for my landlord. True to form, he had harangued them about every conceivable detail of their handywork; maybe they decided to take revenge on him with a little detail of their own. One thing's for sure: I didn't disturb anyone while I was in the summer room. As a writer I lived like a monk. I was especially conscientious about not being noisy – I closed doors quietly and I tip-toed through the garden. Maybe I was too quiet; maybe someone got a fright because they thought I was a burglar.

In any case, I didn't feel much animosity towards whomever it was who reported me to the authorities. My annoyance was focused on the fact that someone from the Council – someone I didn't know and who didn't know me, and who therefore knew nothing about my personal circumstances or my needs – could turn up with a clipboard, scrutinise my private accommodation, for which I was voluntarily paying, and instruct me with the full force of the law to go and live somewhere else, supposedly for my own good. I was outraged. Living in the summer room was in my interests, because I had decided it was in my interests.

That was the beginning and the end of the matter. I didn't need a bureaucrat to tell me what to do with my life. What was next? Someone coming round to tell me what to write in my book?

My landlord was as bemused as I was about the situation – perhaps more so, due to his background. He grew up in Hong Kong, where he would have been perfectly within his rights to let out the summer room. He simply couldn't understand what he had done wrong. And he was distraught that his investment had been in vain; he couldn't afford the expensive planning costs that he would incur if he were to fully equip the building.

I didn't want to get my landlord into trouble, so I spent the next day lugging all my stuff out of the summer room. It poured with rain the whole time, and he buzzed around me in an anorak, showing me the correct way to carry things. There was only one thing to be glad about, which was that the Council's pronouncement was well timed. A few days earlier, one of the tenants in the main house had moved out, and her room was still vacant. I could move my stuff in there straight away, and the rent was the same as what I was already paying. The prospect of living in a shared house again was far from ideal, but it was better than being homeless. I managed to get everything shifted by the end of the afternoon.

But this day of stings had a sting in its tail. In the evening I had to go to work; I was scheduled to do deliveries on my e-bike. I didn't mind cycling in bad weather, only, when it was raining, I needed to remember to wear my contact lenses instead of my glasses. In the event, moving my stuff took me so long I was running late, so I just grabbed my glasses as I rushed out the door. This proved to be a fateful decision. Later that night, in the dark, when I was cycling on a designated cycle track, with the rain still hammering down, and my glasses speckled with water, I had an accident. The Council, in its infinite wisdom, had erected a road sign in the middle of the cycle track. The sign was there to warn motorists of the presence of speed cameras. Because I had cycled on that stretch of pavement so many times, I wasn't expecting an obstacle. I was doing about 20 miles an hour when... whack. My shoulder hit the signpost, and I went sprawling. The e-bike was damaged, and I badly injured my knee. As a consequence I couldn't work for two weeks, so I lost several hundred pounds in earnings, in addition to the hundreds of pounds I had to spend on fixing my bike. Thank goodness I didn't collide with the sign face-first.

All in all, it was a triumphant day for the local council. First they evicted me from my freely chosen home for no reason. Then they assaulted me with a signpost.

11.

I tried to be positive, as ever. There were, after all, a few upsides to living in the main house – central heating, for instance, and a bathroom just across the corridor. I was grateful for these luxuries when, several months after moving in, I caught swine flu, and, not long after that, a vomiting bug.

Even so, I would have preferred to stick it out in the summer room. Now that I was sharing a house with other people again, my stress levels went through the roof (maybe that's why I got sick). There were four of us in the house – myself and two other tenants upstairs, and my landlord downstairs. My room was unique in that it was adjoined by each of the others' rooms, while their rooms were adjoined only by mine. This meant that I was trapped in a sort of secret chamber of noise. Because the others couldn't hear each other's noise, and because they couldn't hear me (because I was quiet), they had no idea how noisy the house was.

In the room to the left of mine was a (not very devout) British Muslim from Rochdale. He had a good job in computing, so in the daytimes he went to work. In the evenings, he typically watched movies or talked to his friends on Skype, often till late. To be fair, he turned out to be a good guy. I enjoyed talking to him when we bumped into each other. After a few weeks, when I had got to know him, I mentioned that sometimes he kept me awake at bedtime. He was instantly apologetic, and he started using headphones while he was watching films, and he cut out the late-night chats.

In the room to the right of mine was a young Estonian man who had finished his undergraduate degree a few months previously. He claimed to be looking for a job in Britain, though I'm not sure how he expected to find one, given that he hardly ever left his room. His noise specialism was playing loud video games constantly, complete with shooting sounds and explosions. Often he played online multiplayer games, which involved him wearing a headset with a microphone through which he chatted inanely to his friends around the world while they played too. He also chatted on the phone to his girlfriend, most evenings, typically sometime between 11pm and 1am. He had an extremely loud, intensely nasal voice that sounded like a vuvuzela; it penetrated the walls like a needle through skin. I asked him if he could be a little quieter, especially at night, but he was unrepentant. He wasn't doing anything wrong, he insisted, because the previous tenant hadn't complained. He refused to budge from this position. No matter what I said, he was convinced that I was being unreasonable, *because the previous tenant hadn't complained.* Some days, I could hear him yelling in his native Russian on the phone. I suspect he was badgering his parents to send him more money. All the while, his room got messier and smellier.

Finally, in the room beneath mine was my landlord. To my consternation, I soon discovered that along with his OCD he suffered from some sort of Tourette's-like condition. I don't wish to be unkind to people who have Tourette's – I have a mild case of it myself – but my landlord's condition involved him making bewildering noises at bewildering times. His symptoms regularly flowered at bedtime. He would cough and splutter and clear his throat and, well, *roar*, for want of a better word. It was like listening to an unusually long Heimlich manoeuvre. Ear plugs were futile. You can't blot out the sound of someone who sounds like they're dying. My landlord was also a prolific late-night phone talker. His wife had left him a few years previously, and he often phoned her to protest his loneliness. He would wail and shout and plead and rant into the early hours.

The more I got to know my landlord, the more I realised he was a deeply troubled man. I felt sorry for him, so I tried to talk to him about his difficulties. He had been unemployed for almost a decade, and he knew he needed to get a job, but he kept insisting that the house would go to rack and ruin if he wasn't around to supervise his tenants. There was no convincing him otherwise. In truth, I think he enjoyed prowling around looking for infractions of the house rules; I think he even enjoyed finding them. The more time I spent in the house, the more I was exposed to his antics. I was hardly permitted to do anything without him standing over me, watching me, advising me. When I was sitting downstairs eating my breakfast, he would suggest that I moved my chair two inches to the left, just in case someone wanted to open the fridge door. When I was cooking pasta, he would monitor the boiling water to ensure it didn't spill over. When I went to the bathroom, he would sneak in there afterwards to inspect the shower cubicle or the toilet bowl.

Inevitably, I started getting into arguments with him. Quite simply, he was the most infuriating man I have ever met. One of the things we argued about was the acceptability of late-night phone conversations in the house. I proposed a new rule: no phone conversations after 11pm. My landlord agreed to my proposal in the end, but he refused to follow the rule himself; he reserved the right to do whatever he wanted in his own home. And when the Estonian broke the rule, which he frequently did, my landlord invariably responded by suggesting that I was being hypersensitive, because *the previous tenant hadn't complained.* I felt powerless and dismayed, as though I was living under a dictatorial regime in which all measures were being taken to promote an agreeable atmosphere apart from any measures that were actually conducive to an agreeable atmosphere. Gradually I realised that my landlord – himself a university graduate – was similar to the kind of philosophically hypochondriacal intellectual from whom I had tried to distance myself ever since my PhD: he was hiding from life, and living comfortably off the efforts of other people, while kidding himself that he was some sort of benevolent overlord. Tellingly, he was sympathetic to communism, even though (or, perhaps I should say, because) he had only ever lived under capitalism; he had emigrated to the UK when Hong Kong was still ruled by the British. He preferred to remain in the UK, he explained, because he was "freer" here than he would be in China. I couldn't get my head around this. He was using his cherished freedom to argue that communism is better than capitalism.

12.

In the summer of 2016, I discovered that self-styled benevolent overlords are even more numerous than I had previously realised. A national debate was taking place prior to a referendum that would determine whether or not the UK would remain in the European Union. Critics of the EU were insisting that it is a corrupt, undemocratic and overly bureaucratic organisation whose leaders – including *five* presidents – are aloof from everyday life but exert a massive and malign influence on British society. The EU, these critics argued, suffocates the economy by inundating businesses and citizens with a rising tide of arbitrary rules and regulations. To me, this sounded like authoritarian socialism, which made me want to vote 'Leave'. But at the same time, I was also being reminded by supporters of the EU that Britain trades prolifically with Europe. To me, this sounded like capitalism, which made me want to vote 'Remain'.

The debates about the EU also drew my attention to an issue I hadn't thought about much: immigration. Up until the EU referendum, I was in the habit of assuming that anyone who said anything negative about immigration was a bad person. My assumption was an example of one of those simplistic slogans that often pass for reasoning among socialists: "immigration is good; critics of immigration are bad." I remember when, a few years earlier, Labour Prime Minister Gordon Brown infamously got into a discussion about immigration with an elderly working-class woman in the street in Rochdale. The woman – Gillian Duffy – told Brown that she was "ashamed" to be a Labour supporter. Reeling off various complaints about the government, she blustered, somewhat inanely: "All these Eastern Europeans what are coming in, where are they flocking from?" After the debate, Brown climbed into the back seat of his big grey car and – unaware that his microphone was still switched on – described Duffy as a "bigoted woman". There was a public outcry. However, at the time, my sympathies were entirely with Brown. I automatically assumed, like him, that the woman was a bigot, no question. That was the end of the matter as far as I was concerned.

By the summer of 2016, this cognitive dead end was perhaps the only remaining legacy of my previous socialist views. As I listened to the debates about the EU, I realised that my self-indulgent sloganeering about immigration had blinded me to any real understanding of the issues. I endeavoured to do my own research. I soon discovered some surprising facts.

Consider the facts about net migration to the UK. Annual net migration is defined as the number of people immigrating to a country minus the number of people emigrating from that country in a year. In the 1960s and 1970s the figure for annual net migration (to the UK) was mostly negative: tens of thousands more people were emigrating than immigrating. In the 1980s and 1990s the figure became positive but remained low: in most years, tens of thousands more people were immigrating than emigrating. Then, in 1998, a massive rise occurred. The annual net migration figure soared above 100,000 then stayed above 150,000 for two decades, exceeding 200,000 for eight years in a row, and peaking at a colossal 336,000 in 2015.

What caused this overall surge in net migration? Numerically speaking, the cause was a rise in immigration. Although concurrently there was a moderate increase in emigration, the UK welcomed roughly half a million immigrants each year during that two-decade period. Let me repeat and refine that statistic: for the last twenty years, the UK has opened its doors to an average of almost 550,000 immigrants per year. When people talk about the UK's 'mass immigration', they are referring to this period, during which there was, well, a massive level of immigration, a level unprecedented in the history of the British Isles. Often, indeed, when British people today use the word 'immigration' at all they are referring to mass immigration; they intend to be understood in the context of recent years. Another thing that should be noted is that these figures don't include illegal immigration, which for obvious reasons is difficult to measure. In 2009, the London School of Economics estimated that there are 725,000 illegal immigrants in Britain.

Mass immigration to the UK happened because of deliberate political decisions. When New Labour came to power in 1997 they loosened the rules on immigration. Andrew Neather, a former speechwriter for the party, has recalled that Tony Blair's government wanted to attract more immigrants to the UK so as 'to rub the right's nose in diversity and render their arguments out of date'. The second part of Neather's explanation hints at another probable motive for New Labour's legislative support for mass immigration: they wanted to enlarge the electoral constituency for the left, immigrants generally being poorer than non-immigrants. Moreover, New Labour were probably confident that their supporters would help bring about this enlargement, by relentlessly telling immigrants that the only people who care about them are socialists, everyone else in British society supposedly being xenophobic and bigoted. Tellingly, Barbara Roche, who was Minister for Asylum and Immigration during Blair's first term, declared that the immigration constraints of the day were 'racist'. The left's overall policy of facilitating immigration while stoking grievances among immigrants has been particularly impactful in regard to Muslims. In 1991, there were 950,000 Muslims in Britain; today there are an estimated 4.13 million. Like my landlord's girlfriend in Cambridge, most Muslims lean to the left polit-ically. In the 2017 general election, 85% of British Muslims voted Labour.

Of course, another major cause of the recent surge in immigration was Britain's membership of the EU. In 1992 the UK government, without consulting the public, signed the Maastricht Treaty, which created the European Union and the concept of 'European citizenship'. The principle of 'free movement' gave European citizens the right to live and work, visa-free, anywhere within the EU. Hence, as more and more countries joined the EU – including, in 2004, eight former communist countries – more and more people became eligible to move to the UK. Today, the total number of EU citizens is approximately 500 million.

Over the last two decades, approximately a quarter of the people who immigrated to the UK came from EU countries.

At the same time, the EU has made it easier for migrants from around the world to come to the UK. EU countries can unilaterally accept any number of immigrants, and, once those immigrants are European citizens, they can move around the continent at will. Moreover, in the last few decades, EU countries with borders near, or onto, non-EU countries have struggled to manage an unprecedented level of illegal migration. If, upon arriving at the EU's border states, illegal immigrants declare that their aim is to move to someplace else within the continent, there is an incentive for the border authorities to admit those immigrants rather than spend a large amount of money processing them. Naturally, the UK is an especially attractive destination for migrants; our economy is the fourth largest in the world, and English is the *lingua franca* of the world. Hence, the UK has become a lightning rod for illegal migration into the EU. For the same reason, the UK has also become a lightning rod for people who migrate legally into the EU. If migrants wish to come to the UK, they simply need to target an EU country with a relatively lax immigration policy, and use that country as a staging post.

There has been a lot of debate about how many of the UK's immigrants – whether from the EU or beyond – came here solely to access our generous welfare system. I'm sure you've heard some disturbing stories about so-called 'benefits tourism'. Here's one from me: a couple of years ago I did some delivery shifts for a takeaway business run by Bangladeshis who told me of several members of their community who were living off the welfare state while also deriving a rental income from properties they owned in Spain. However, despite anecdotes such as these, the full extent of the problem of benefits tourism is not known.

What is clear is that mass immigration has cost the UK money. In 2014 the Centre for Research and Analysis of Migration at University College London published a paper called 'The Fiscal Effects of Immigration to the UK'. The paper estimated that between the years 1995 and 2011 UK immigrants received (in benefits and other services) over a hundred billion pounds more than they paid to the Exchequer in taxes: in other words, mass immigration has cost the UK over a hundred billion pounds. Interestingly, the report separated out the figures for EEA immigrants and non-EEA immigrants (the EEA is the EU plus Norway, Iceland and Lichtenstein). While non-EEA immigrants had cost the Exchequer £118 billion pounds, EEA immigrants had actually made a net contribution – of £4.4 billion pounds. You often hear about the 'economic benefits' of EU free movement; that modest figure is one of them.

Mass immigration has, however, come with other downsides. Many of these downsides are the consequence of an obvious problem: overcrowding. The UK's public services in particular have been compromised by the extra demand placed on them. For instance, we've all heard that the NHS is in 'crisis'. Despite continual increases in government health spending, the NHS has struggled with the practicalities of treating so many newcomers. In 2015/16 alone, there were almost 745,000 new migrant GP registrations – a record number – in England, Wales and

Northern Ireland. As well as bringing this weight of numbers, there are concerns that mass immigration is driving an increase in incidences of three serious infectious diseases: Aids, hepatitis and tuberculosis. The London Communicable Diseases Surveillance Centre has recommended that the UK follows other countries, including Australia, Canada, Spain, Singapore and the US, in conducting 'new entrant screening'. Meanwhile, in 2016, almost a third of all births in the UK were to foreign-born women, a rate that has been increasing since 1990. The increase is partly due to the higher fertility rates of immigrant women, but also due to the fact that immigrants are more likely than non-immigrants to be of child-bearing age.

Schools, too, are struggling to cope with mass immigration. Recent statistics reveal a growing problem with overcrowding in secondary schools in England: in the last two years, two thirds of secondary schools have reported an increase in class sizes, and, in the five years before that, there was a threefold increase in the number of children taught in classes of 36 or more. Overall, 40% of secondary schools in England are full or overcrowded, according to one report. Statistics also suggest that primary school class sizes have been increasing throughout Britain. Granted, in the last few years the situation in Britain's schools hasn't been helped by a slight reduction in education funding (followed by a plateau), but overall there has been a huge increase in government spending on education in the last few decades. In any case, the negative effects of mass immigration on schools are not just numerical. Today, in England, at least 1.1 million schoolchildren speak English as a second language, and there are 240 schools where over 90% of pupils do so; astonishingly, there are five primary schools where the number of pupils who speak English as a first language is *zero*. Overall, in *one in nine* schools in England a majority of pupils do not speak English as their first language. Naturally, children who can't speak fluent English require special attention, which makes life harder for their teachers and for the other pupils in the school. And there is a financial cost involved here too: in 2015/16, the government allocated £267 million to schools to help foreign pupils with their English.

From 2001 to 2016, immigration added at least 5.4 million people to the UK's population (when you also factor in children born to at least one immigrant parent). An enormous and completely unrealistic investment in infrastructure – in roads and public transport as well as in health and education – would have been necessary in order to keep up with such a huge inflow of people. And, of course, mass immigration has been a key factor in the housing crisis. Overcrowding has overwhelmed the UK's capacity to house its inhabitants. Consider the figure for net migration in 2015. To accommodate 336,000 new people, the UK would have needed to build, in one year, a city bigger than Newcastle. In turn, every year for the past twenty years, the UK would have needed to build other new cities, just to keep pace with net migration. Twenty new cities in twenty years? It's madness. In the year after the Brexit vote, net migration dropped to 230,000. Many pundits talked plaintively about a 'Brexodus'. Well, no, it wasn't anything of the sort. It was still a positive figure for net migration – including a positive figure for net migration from the EU. (Annual net migration, remember, is defined as the number of people immigrating to a country minus the number of people emigrating from that country in a year.) And the negative impact of this population increase could only have been offset by the (hypothetical) building of another new city, complete with new hospitals, scores of new schools, and new roads and transport links.

Naturally, mass immigration has impacted most heavily on the UK's poorest people, who are bearing the brunt of the crises in public services and housing. Poor people can't afford private health insurance; they have no choice but to tolerate long waiting times and attenuated care in the NHS. Poor people can't afford private education, or a house in the catchment area of a sought-after state school; they have no choice but to send their children to a bog-standard state school where the class sizes are huge and many of the pupils speak in broken English. Indeed, poor people can't afford to buy a house on the private market at all, and, if they request a council house, they will have to join a waiting list that has been lengthened by mass immigration. And, all the while, immigrants are pushing down the wages of poor people by flooding the market for unskilled labour.

Of course, many immigrants are poor, too. But the crucial difference is: they have generally become richer by immigrating to Britain, whereas the British poor have generally become poorer through mass immigration. Consider so-called 'work tourists' – immigrants who come to Britain temporarily to earn a better living than they can at home – the typical example being a young person from a former communist country. In the short term, work tourists don't mind living in cramped shared accommodation in an overcrowded country; the sacrifice is worth it, because they'll soon return home much richer than they would have been if they'd never departed. On their return, armed with the superior spending power of the pound, they'll be in a position to buy a house and start a family near their own families, and live happily ever after. In contrast, the British poor with whom the work tourists compete for jobs and houses have bleaker prospects. For the British poor, there's no pot of gold at the end of the rainbow. They'll struggle to save enough money to buy a house in Britain. And they can't turn the water of their meagre earnings into the wine of a better life someplace else. They can't realistically decamp to, say, Bulgaria or Romania, away from their families and their culture, and nor do they want to. Their real life, their only life, is here. They, too, might want to start a family. But they can hardly do it while living in a single room in a cramped shared house. Indeed, while they attempt to grind out some sort of viable future for themselves, they might even have to share a house with work tourists, whose lifestyles are likely to reflect a more carefree outlook. This really brings home the reality of the situation: not only are the British poor worse off than work tourists, but they are sacrificing precious opportunities so as to make work tourists richer.

Things are admittedly different when it comes to immigrants from very poor countries. Many of these immigrants aren't so much work tourists as people who come to Britain to make a permanent home here (although they may at the same time send money back to their country of origin). It is impossible not to feel a measure of sympathy for these migrants, especially if they are suffering from health conditions. But the point is: whereas sympathy for poverty-stricken migrants is near-universal, the sacrifices made in the name of such sympathy are not universally shared. The wealthier the British citizen, the less they are affected by mass immigration. Bear this in mind when you hear supporters of mass immigration insisting that they want to live in a country that is 'open to the world'. Unless these people are personally making significant sacrifices in the name of mass immigration, they are in fact expecting Britain's poor to pick up the tab.

Indeed, as Andrew Neather hinted, many comfortably off people in Britain are benefitting financially from mass immigration. People whose salaries are paid directly or indirectly by the government – whether bureaucrats, academics, social workers, lawyers or left-wing journalists – are benefitting from a huge increase in the number of government dependents; the more help is needed, the more the helpers and their associates are needed. At the same time, mass immigration is also benefitting the government's associates in the commercial sector. The leaders of big businesses often collude with the government over various issues, mass immigration being an example; a large inflow of unskilled workers provides plentiful cheap labour. By drawing generous salaries, courtesy of the monopolistic power of the state, the various beneficiaries of mass immigration ensure that they themselves are protected against the problem of overcrowding. Like all comfortably-off people, they can afford to buy a house. They can to afford to privately educate their children, or to buy a house in the catchment area of a good state school. They can afford private healthcare. They may even have private health insurance cover as part of their salaries. British poor people are making sacrifices not only on behalf of immigrants, but on behalf of the comfortably-off British 'elites' for whom mass immigration is a gravy train.

When the EU referendum was in full swing, I got into a conversation about the topic with a fellow writer. Being a *bien pensant* type, she told me that of course she is in favour of mass immigration (and diversity and multiculturalism and all that). But moments later, I had reason to doubt her sincerity. In an apparent change of subject, she started talking about her daughter's education. Her daughter, she said happily, had been offered a place at a good state school where the other children were – I quote – "from nice middle-class families". *Lucky for some*, I remember thinking.

Some people have an empathy blind spot when it comes to the impact of mass immigration on Britain's poor. Amid all the moral grandstanding about immigration, an important question has often been overlooked: do Britain's poor people *want* to make enormous sacrifices so that their country can be 'open to the world'? When this question was finally asked officially, albeit by proxy, by way of the EU referendum, the answer was clear. Yet for many supporters of mass immigration the blind spot remained. They refused to accept the validity of the answer they had heard. Before and after the vote, poor people who offered negative opinions on immigration were tarred as stupid, narrowminded, xenophobic, or racist. This callous and condescending reaction was unfair in many ways. For a start, it failed to recognise that there is a difference between complaining about mass immigration and complaining about immigration per se. If immigration had remained at sensible levels, British poor people would have suffered less, and far fewer of them would have complained.

Likewise, there is a difference between complaining about excessive immigration and complaining about immigrants – a difference that is frequently over-looked, albeit rarely by the complainants themselves. Excessive immigration is a matter of numbers; immigrants are people. Logically, you can complain that there are too many immigrants and make no comment at all about immigrants themselves. You can, indeed, complain that there are too many immigrants and also point out that many immigrants have undoubtedly made a positive contribution to the UK. Even if *all* the immigrants – each and every one of them – who came to the UK in the last twenty years had been paragons of virtue, saintly figures who brought light and love and wisdom to all who crossed their paths, there would still have been legitimate concerns about how to provide so many newcomers with housing, healthcare, schooling and other services without seriously compromising the opportunities available to the existing British population, especially those on low incomes.

And – on that note – another troubling aspect of the national discussion about immigration is that any criticism of immigrants, any criticism at all, seems to have become beyond the pale in so-called polite society. Of course, taking a dislike to someone purely because they are an immigrant, or because they are a member of a particular immigrant community, is spiteful and contemptible. Of course, making blanket condemnations of all immigrants, or of particular immigrant communities, is spiteful and contemptible.

And, of course, deliberately saying dishonest things about immigrants is spiteful and contemptible. But honest criticism of immigrants is not spiteful and contemptible. There is nothing wrong with attempting to tell the truth – including the moral truth – about people. In fact, it would be spiteful and contemptible *not* to allow immigrants to be subjected to (honest) criticism. To exempt them from criticism would be to treat them as unworthy of standards that are applied to non-immigrants. Indeed, one of the main reasons people criticise immigrants is precisely that some immigrants have made outsiders of themselves. Some immigrants have made no effort to assimilate to British life or to learn English, and some immigrant communities have been overrepresented in certain types of crime. Criticisms such as these are implicit calls for unity, not disunity.

And, anyway, it's not as though we're always unwilling to criticise foreigners – when the roles are reversed. We're all accustomed to criticising the behaviour of Brits abroad, whether they're football hooligans fighting in foreign cities, drunken revellers urinating, vomiting and performing sex acts in the streets of Ibiza, or ex-pats (or even ex-cons) holing themselves up in insular British communities on the Costa d'el Sol. We're also accustomed to talking about the misbehaviour, when it occurs, of foreign people in their own countries. No one in Britain, immigrants included, should be beyond reproach. No one deserves to be silenced for offering honest criticism.

Indeed, we should always react attentively to criticism of immigrants precisely because if the people who are making the allegations are mistaken then only a reasoned response is likely to change their minds.

Silencing the critics is only likely to succeed in compounding their sense of injustice, and perhaps even pushing them towards extremists – genuine racists and political lunatics – by whom the critics feel they are being taken seriously. And let us remember that when immigrants behave in a way that has a negative effect on a neighbourhood, the people who bear the brunt of this behaviour are likely to be poor, because immigrants tend to move into poorer areas. For many British poor people, bad behaviour by immigrants feels like salt rubbed into the wound of the housing crisis. Poor people who express concerns about immigrants deserve to be treated with no less empathy than immigrants themselves.

The truth is, the vast majority of British people, including poor people, have treated immigrants with empathy, courtesy and tolerance, as is British custom. Most of the people – including some immigrants themselves – who have expressed concerns about immigration have done so in a legitimate way. The same goes for most of the politicians and campaigners who have spoken out on behalf of their concerned compatriots. But reputations are not always deserving. As I listened to people debating the EU during the referendum – and as I participated in a few such debates myself – I was dismayed to see so many Remainers levelling accusations of bigotry at people who were attempting to be honest about immigration. Even people who criticised the EU as an institution were often – unfairly – accused of xenophobia. I was particularly dismayed at the way Nigel Farage was treated. Almost every time he appeared in public to defend the reasonable views of tens of millions of his fellow Britons, he was sneered at and bullied, his opponents shouting hackneyed slogans at him rather than engaging with the points he was making. Just as I was pushed away from socialism by socialists, I was pushed away from my instinctive support for the EU by supporters of the EU. (Indeed, many Remainers *were* socialists; 65% of Labour supporters were Remainers, compared to 39% of Tories.)

Some Remainers even went as far as calling Leavers 'fascists'. This awful slur, it seems to me, gets things entirely back to front. I do not mean that the EU is a fascist organisation, or that its supporters are fascists – that would be going way, way too far. What I mean is that the worldview of most Leavers is comparable to that of the stoical Westerners who, in the middle of the twentieth century, stood firm when most of Europe was under the shadow of totalitarianism. The preservation of agreed borders, the distaste for the idea that the common good is served by government-engineered population upheavals, the preference for internationalism over supranationalism, the rights of peoples to self-determination, the inviolability of democracy, the protection of individual rights, the rejection of anti-capitalist governance, the love of freedom – freedom of speech, freedom of association, freedom of religion, freedom of economic activity – and the belief that rigorous open debate should triumph over the enforcement of arbitrary taboos: these were the reasons most Leavers voted the way they did. At bottom, most Leavers simply wanted to do the right thing. This verdict is supported by one of the most interesting but little-known studies of voters during the referendum: in personality tests devised by psychologists, Leavers tended to display higher levels of *conscientiousness* than Remainers.

And no doubt many of the people who voted Leave just wanted a decent house to live in, at a reasonable cost. Around the time of the referendum, I had a conversation with my landlord about the EU. He told me he was voting Remain, because mass immigration was pushing up the value of his house and enabling him to derive an easy income on the back of a plentiful supply of tenants. *Lucky for some*, I remember thinking. I voted Leave – in more ways than one, it turned out.

13.

My sister once gave me a piece of advice that I've never forgotten. She said there are three main areas of your life – your personal relationships, your home life, and your work life – and each of these areas can go wrong. You can cope with any one of these areas going wrong at any time, she said, but if two of them go wrong simultaneously, you'll struggle to cope. She never told me what would happen if all three went wrong simultaneously. I was about to find out.

By the summer of 2016 my home life had become a pantomime. I was like a fugitive in my own house, forever trying to avoid my landlord and his day-ruining annoyingness, but never able to avoid his irksome knock on my bedroom door if I ever left so much as a crumb on a kitchen surface. Meanwhile, in the bedroom next door to mine, the Estonian was being as noisy as ever. Sometimes I would hammer my fist on the adjoining wall, sometimes on his door, in a futile effort to get him to shut up. We would shout at each other, swearing and catcalling like a couple of tramps, until my landlord or the guy in the other room intervened. The confrontation would usually end with me grudgingly accepting that everyone had a right to make some noise during the daytime. But when the Estonian was noisy late in the evenings, I reckoned I had a right to retaliate. The next morning I would go out of the house early and leave my iPad on, playing YouTube videos of 'annoying noises' on full volume in my room (yes, there are plenty of such videos online, perfectly exemplifying the fact that the internet is both amazing and ludicrous). The Muslim guy from Rochdale had already left for work – I made sure of this – but the Estonian was usually still trying to sleep. I soon noticed that he was being quieter late in the evenings – a success! Alas, my tit-for-tat strategy didn't last long because my landlord started complaining about the strange noises coming from my room. Talk about the pot calling the kettle black.

As for my personal relationships... well, I had got into so many bitter arguments about politics with my friends that I didn't have many personal relationships left. I say 'arguments': in fact these interactions didn't involve arguments in the logicians' sense of people criticising each other's premises, conclusions or inferences. Rather, my premises, conclusions and inferences were being used as a basis for severe criticism of me personally. My best friend from university stormed off in a huff when I told him I wasn't in favour of a socialist revolution. "You've no idea what you're talking about; this is the worst night I've ever had," was the last thing he said to me. My best friend from secondary school also stormed off in a huff when I explained to him some of the reasons I wasn't a supporter of Jeremy Corbyn. "You annoy everyone you talk to," was my friend's (probably accurate) departing comment.

My evening job became a sort of sanctuary for me – which was an unexpected outcome, to say the least. During the many years that I've worked as a delivery driver, at various restaurants, I've been in some dodgy situations and I've met some even dodgier characters. I reckon about a third of the people who order take-aways for delivery are on welfare, and rarely for a legitimate reason. With the taxpayer paying for their dinner, their house, and the bringing of their dinner to their house, my customers have summoned me to some bleak council estates. I've been shouted at, or threatened, or chased, by people who were angry because their food was late, or cold, or not what they ordered, or because I knocked too loudly. I've delivered to druggies who could barely stand up, the stench of dope wafting out of their open door. I've been propositioned on the doorstep by scantily clad drunken women. I've seen customers having sex, in full view through the living room window, the woman jumping off the sofa and hitching up her dress before opening the front door and greeting me with an innocent smile. I've seen fights among drunken cust-omers outside the restaurant, including an epic brawl involving scores of men (and a few women). I've arrived back from a delivery to find that three of my colleagues have been arrested for jumping over the counter brandishing kebab knives and chasing a violent customer down the street. I've arrived back from a delivery to find that one of the kitchen staff has been bundled into a van by the immigration auth-orities. I've met lots of fellow drivers who were on benefits but who were illegally earning extra money on the side.

I've met a driver, six foot six tall and built like a wrestler, who had recently been released from prison where he'd been serving a sentence for "violent offences". He was actually a very a nice bloke – until he lost his temper. One evening he got into a heated argument with one of our colleagues. A little later I went out into the yard and I found him – the driver – pacing up and down clapping his fist into his palm. "I'm going to kill him," he kept saying. Obviously, I tried to talk him out of it, reminding him that he'd go back to prison for murder. "Yes," he said, "but it'll be worth it because I'll *enjoy* killing him. I'll lock him in the back of my van and beat the crap out of him, then I'll drive him into the woods and drill a hole in his back, and when the fat oozes out, I'll set fire to him like a candle." Needless to say, I hadn't been trained for this kind of situation. Luckily, somehow, my words of consolation did the trick for once. The ex-con decided to remain an ex-con; he screeched off in his car and didn't come back.

So I've seen a lot of crazy stuff at my various delivery jobs, but mostly I've avoided getting personally involved in the craziness. Unfortunately, in summer 2016, that changed. There were two main troublemakers in our restaurant, and they were increasingly causing problems because the owners of the company were increasingly taking a backseat role, leaving other staff members in charge during service. One of the troublemakers was the delivery manager, who was responsible for taking orders on the phone and packaging up the deliveries. He was an arrogant man, partly because of his senior position, but also, I suspect, because he had been on benefits all his adult life. He had been diagnosed with Asperger Syndrome when he was a kid, and as an adult this entitled him to receive income support and free rent in perpetuity. He lived in a flat in one of the nicest parts of town with his lover who was registered as his 'carer', a role which also came with a financial payment, despite the fact that they both worked full time. It struck me that my delivery manager's longstanding insulation from the pressures of life had turned him into a spoilt brat. He was bitchy and manipulative, never taking responsibility for anything. He was always arguing with other staff members and blaming them for his own mistakes. On a typical night we had four drivers and three cyclists on the delivery team, so there were plenty of candidates for him to bully. He would pick a particular person and relentlessly slag them off behind their back, and nag them to their face. Inevitably, this would lead to flare-ups, his victims protesting their mistreatment. A succession of them stormed out furiously, never to be seen again.

The other troublemaker was the chef. He was an Egyptian Muslim who had spent most of his life in Italy. He was very devout; every now and then he would abandon his duties in the kitchen because he had to perform his prayer rituals in the backroom. When things went wrong, which they inevitably did, he was quick to get angry. I was tempted to add 'like all chefs', but in my experience this stereotype is inaccurate. Gordon Ramsey notwithstanding, most chefs are calm and methodical in their dealings with other staff members; in a pressurised environment, politeness is the best policy. Unfortunately, our chef was not like most chefs. During any controversy he would wave his arms around and shout in machine-gun Italian. The only way to get him to calm down was to back down; as a result, no problem could ever be solved constructively, because every problem became the tangential problem of placating the chef. This dysfunctional dynamic wasn't helped by the fact that most of the other kitchen staff were Italian, handpicked by the chef. They didn't speak good enough English to be able to understand anyone other than him, so any query with any subordinate member of the kitchen staff was soon deferred to the chef, which led to more shouty handwaving. After a while, I formed the impression that the chef's religious piety was an exacerbating factor rather than a mitigating factor in his diva-like behaviour. His devotion to Allah was acting as a sort of moral get-out-of-jail free card for him; after he had paid his dues in prayer, he could behave with impunity towards his colleagues. He, too, kept antagonising people to the point when they stormed out in protest. We had a high staff turnover.

I suppose it was inevitable that the chef and the delivery manager would come to blows at some point, and come to blows they did. I can't deny experiencing a sense of schadenfreude when it happened. The delivery manager must have said something out of turn, because suddenly, in the corner of my eye, I saw the chef hurl something at him; a pile of foil trays went flying over the kitchen counter, some of them clattering into the delivery manager's head, the others slamming against the back wall. For a moment, it was unclear which of these two untouchable antagonists would back down. But only for a moment. The delivery manager meekly bent down and picked up the scattered trays from the floor. Then he went outside for a cigarette and a moan.

I suppose it was also inevitable that I would come to blows with these two troublemakers. First in line was the delivery manager. To be honest I can't remember what we argued about. But it was a serious enough incident to come to the attention of the owners of the company. To my surprise, they responded by asking me if I wanted to be promoted – into the delivery manager's job. He was to remain with the company, but in a lesser role. I accepted, partly because I wanted to help the owners out, and partly because they were offering me more money; I could earn as much in four days as I could in six. For a while, this appeared to be a good arrangement. The atmosphere in the restaurant improved, and my own life improved. With a few extra nights off, I was less tired, and I was able to work more intensely on my writing during the daytimes.

Unfortunately, the good atmosphere in the restaurant didn't last. In one fell swoop, I managed to antagonise almost everyone in the kitchen. The catalyst for the row was a discussion I had had with the owners about cost-cutting. They were very stressed out because, despite their brand being popular in Cambridge, they weren't making much money. The local authority was charging an extortionate amount of business tax, which was eating into their profits, as was the exorbitant cost of renting the business premises. This is another seldom remarked-on aspect of the housing crisis. Running a small business is difficult at the best of times, let alone when there's a mountain of rent to climb every month because there are so few affordable premises, because buildings are in such short supply. The situation was reaching a crisis point for my employers; they had bills to pay at home, and children to feed. So I made a suggestion: perhaps we could save money by reducing staff hours on the delivery side. For the first half hour of service, when the restaurant was invariably very quiet, I wondered if the kitchen staff could answer the telephone and take orders. The orders could be fulfilled as soon as the delivery team arrived half an hour later; after all, the food needed to be cooked before it could be delivered. This small alteration would save thousands of pounds each year.

My suggestion went against my own interests. As a member of the delivery team, I would work fewer hours and earn less if it was implemented. But to my surprise, when the owners broached the idea with all the other staff members, it was the kitchen staff who complained. They didn't want to take on any extra 'responsibilities' without being paid more. I thought this was lame, given that the extra responsibilities would only involve occasionally answering the telephone and taking a few customer orders. Without this miniscule sacrifice, the business was heading down the drain, but without the cooperation of the chef and his team, my suggestion wasn't taken up. I couldn't believe it. I had completely misjudged the situation. A few days later, I became aware of how much animosity my suggestion had generated. One of the cyclists, an admirable young Sri Lankan man who was studying for a Master's degree at Anglia Ruskin University, took me aside and gave me a warning. He said: "I heard the kitchen staff and the previous delivery manager talking about you behind your back. They *hate* you." He added: "You should watch out for him [the previous manager]; some people get ahead in life by being helpful; others get ahead by cutting other people down." These were wise – and prophetic – words.

In truth, I wasn't surprised to hear that the delivery manager hated me; after all, I had taken his job, and I knew he was likely to seek revenge, because he was a bully. But I was shocked to hear that the kitchen staff apparently hated me too. The next week, I found out just how much. It was a busy night, with around 100 orders to fulfil. Everything was going smoothly, barring one small incident when I had to remind the previous delivery manager of his new role. As agreed with the owners, his role was to help with the packing, never to hand out delivery bags to the drivers and cyclists; now that I was delivery manager, I was solely responsible for checking each delivery before it left the kitchen. He had sent out a bag without my permission, so I politely reminded him not to do that. It wasn't a big deal, so I didn't think any more of it. But 15 minutes later, it came back to haunt me. We were missing some food items – some samosas. I informed the chef, who informed me that he had already cooked them. I said I hadn't seen them on my side of the counter. He said he had definitely cooked them. At the time, I had no idea where the samosas had gone. Later, I realised that they had almost certainly been packed into the wrong bag by the previous delivery manager – the bag he had sent out without my permission. But in the meantime I was simply confused. And I could sense that the chef was dangerously close to a meltdown.

"I'm really sorry," I said, "but you'll have to cook two more samosas."

"Why are you saying I haven't cooked them?" he barked.

"I'm not," I replied. "I'm saying I haven't seen them."

He didn't seem to appreciate this logical distinction, because he suddenly produced a Tupperware box full of cold samosas from a compartment behind him, and started removing them from the box, one by one, slapping them loudly on the work surface, counting as he did so.

"One, two, three, four, five, six, seven, eight... If I haven't cooked the samosas, why are there only eight left in this box?"

"I didn't say you haven't cooked them."

"So where are they then?"

"I don't know; that's my point; I haven't seen them."

"Are you telling me I don't know what's going on in my own kitchen?"

"No, I'm not. Maybe we should talk about this later, not during service."

"I don't need to talk to you about what happens in my kitchen."

"Actually, you do, because we need to work together."

Fair enough, you might think. I certainly thought so. Alas, the chef didn't. He had decided that the time for discussion was over (if the foregoing exchange could be described as a 'discussion'). I saw him reaching downwards... his hand moving towards the dreaded foil trays. I managed to duck just in time before about 30 trays hit the wall behind my head.

I suppose no one really knows how they'll react when an angry little fat man throws a pile of trays at their head from close range. But still my reaction surprised me: I morphed into my school teacher persona. I wagged my finger at the chef and in the most officious voice I could muster I instructed him to come and clear up this mess so we could get on with our jobs. However, he was not a good pupil. His hand reached down again, and this time he picked up a proper (porcelain) plate, and he shaped his body as though he was going to hurl the plate at me like a frisbee. This was a worrying escalation. My reaction became somewhat less pedagogical.

"Don't even think about it."

Unfortunately, the chef deemed this response threatening enough to warrant him striding round the counter and squaring up to me – forehead to forehead. "What are you going to do?" he spat. It was a good question, and the answer suddenly became very clear to me: I wasn't going to do anything. A sense of calm, of complete indifference, came over me like a cool breeze. What I said next was as much a mantra to myself as a message to the chef.

"I don't want to fight you over some samosas."

The chef, however, was very keen to fight. He marched around me, and out into the front yard, where I kept my bicycle. Walking straight over to my bike, he picked it up and hurled it out onto the driveway. He must have known this would rile me – and indeed it did. I lost my cool for a moment. I didn't threaten him or encroach upon him physically, but I uttered a string of sweary insults in his direction. Hearing this, he came towards me with his fists swinging. But he wasn't a very good puncher. It was like being attacked by a potato with little stubby protrusions. I blocked his punches with my palms, and – well, I started laughing.

"You're pathetic," I said.

By this stage, a few of the kitchen staff had come out into the yard, and they were standing around watching the whole incident unfold. Though the chef was obviously the aggressor, our colleagues did nothing to restrain him. He turned round and picked up a broom that was resting on the wall, then he swung the handle at my head. This time, I wasn't laughing. I put my arm up to protect my face, and he smashed the handle down repeatedly on my elbow and forearm. Then he stormed back into the kitchen.

I followed him back in there, for some reason. I guess I didn't want the owners to think I had abandoned my job during service. And – let's be honest – I am invincibly stubborn. Once again, I started lecturing the chef about clearing up the mess. He was being childish, so I figured he deserved to be treated like a child. But when he turned and picked up a huge metal spoon from the work surface behind him, and started striding towards me, I knew it was time to throw in the towel. I walked out into the yard and scooped up my forlorn bike. The last thing I heard as I pedalled away from the restaurant was the previous delivery manager shouting "fuck off, you fucking cunt" as he stood in the open doorway. I guess that's what you call having the last word.

Naturally, I went to the police station – I went straight there, in fact. Over the next few days the police took pictures of the enormous bruise that came out on my arm, and they interviewed the chef and the other kitchen staff, as well as the previous delivery manager. The chef said – falsely – that I had attacked him first. I didn't lay a finger on him, not even in self-defence. And the others said – falsely – that they hadn't seen the incident. Without any evidence, the police said they couldn't take the matter further. Still, I was confident that the owners would back my word over the chef's. And they did – but they said they couldn't sack him because he was indispensable to the business. They asked me if I wanted to keep my job. I said no, of course I don't – not unless I receive an apology from the chef, an apology he was never going to offer, having lied to the police.

So I lost my job. And a few weeks later, the business closed down. I'm not sure what the moral of the story is.

But there's always a silver lining. Perhaps that was the moral. To begin with, I furiously ruminated about the injustice of the situation, but soon I made the most of my newfound free time by surging towards the finishing line of *Scapegoated Capitalism*. Coincidentally, the Estonian had returned to his homeland for about a month, so the house was much quieter than usual. Added to this, I had ample motivation to finish the book quickly, because I had signed a contract with the publisher of my first book to write another book. The new book was to be called *Mindfulness and the Big Questions: Philosophy for Now*. I suppose you might think it peculiar that I would embark on writing another book about mindfulness, what with all the chaos and conflict going on in my life. But the truth is, mindfulness has been helpful to me over the years. Calmly paying attention to my breathing has helped me to cope with the ongoing chaos, and to regain my focus after each of the many rows I've had. It has also helped me to stay calm during those rows. I have never believed that mindfulness is a recipe for passivity. Yes, the whole point of being mindful is to avoid getting carried away by your thoughts and emotions. But mindfulness can also help you to stay firm and fair when *other people* are getting carried away by *their* thoughts and emotions. In other words: mindfulness is the antidote not only to one's own wantonness but to the wantonness of others.

At the end of the autumn of 2016, I finally finished

Scapegoated Capitalism. Without a break, I immediately knuckled down on *Mindfulness and the Big Questions*. However, there were storm clouds on the horizon again. More than ever, I needed to work from home because, during the formative stages of a new manuscript, I needed easy access to all my books and notes. But by now the Estonian had returned to the house, and he was up to his old tricks again. In fact, he had upped the ante. He had found a paid job which he was able to do from his bedroom. From what I could gather, this bizarre job involved him making cartoon-like silly voices for computer games. He had to record little speeches and send them off to a company somewhere. That's about as much as I understood from what he told me. The rest of the time, he played computer games, and chatted to his friends and his girlfriend on Skype – the usual routine. To escape from him, I started doing my writing downstairs at the dining room table. But this meant I was vulnerable to the attentions of my landlord who, as ever, ratted around me like a malfunctioning robot. My stress levels climbed day by day, until finally, one day, I snapped.

I was working in the dining room when my landlord came in and asked me to remove my laptop from the table.

"Why?" I asked.

"Because it's unhygienic."

"Why?"

"Because your laptop has been on your bedroom floor."

"But I don't wear shoes in my bedroom."

"You walk barefoot in there." This was true.

"OK, so why haven't you mentioned this before?"

"I mentioned it when you first came to the house." (He probably did.)

"Then why wasn't it a problem yesterday? And the day before? Has anyone become ill from cross-contamination due to my laptop being on the table?"

"No, but they might do."

"Can I wipe the bottom of my laptop? To make sure it is clean enough for the table? Can I wipe the table after I have used it?"

"I don't want you to do your writing at the dining table."

"OK, so that's what this is about. Where else shall I write? I can't work in my room, because the Estonian guy is up there, making a noise like a chicken."

"He is doing his work."

"But he is always noisy."

"The previous tenant didn't complain."

And with that, my landlord laid the last straw on my creaking back. I snapped. There and then, I told him I wanted to move out. Immediately.

"You can't," he said. "You need to give me a month's notice."

"The contract I signed is void – it was for the summer room."

"Then I won't return your deposit."

"OK," I said, "then I will inform the Council that you rented the summer room to me for six months."

Yes, yes, I know, that was a low blow. It was an especially scurrilous move on my part, given my own feelings about the outrageous Beds in Sheds rule. But I was utterly fed up by this point. And I knew how much my punctilious landlord feared the authorities. For that reason my threat worked. He agreed that I could move out within 24 hours. I immediately went online to look for a new place to live, and I made a few phone calls. Soon I had a plan. The next morning, I dropped off most of my possessions at a lock-up in Cambridge. Then I sped out of town in my car. Mindfully? Probably not. But it was time for a change of scene.

14.

You've probably never heard of the place I drove to: Mickleton, a remote northern village in the hills, 30 miles to the west of Durham. I knew this area quite well, from my days as a student at Durham University, when I used to go on drives into the countryside with my then girlfriend. All these years later, I knew that the wild, romantic landscape of the Durham Dales would give me the inspiration I needed to work on my new book.

When I arrived in Mickleton, I made a phone call to an estate agent, who gave me directions to a property: a little barn on the village outskirts, on a narrow country lane surrounded by fields and hills. Shortly afterwards, a man turned up with a fob of keys to show me around. Like something from a bygone age, the barn was a stumpy grey-stone dwelling fixed like a barnacle onto the rugged slope of the land. The windows and doors were hidden behind heavy wooden shutters. I sensed that no one had been in there for a while. The estate agent released the padlocks, pulled the shutters back, turned a key in a rusty lock, and opened a creaking front door to reveal a shadowy interior that exhaled a blast of musty cold into the autumn air outside. He reached round to press a light switch and in we went.

To my surprise, the barn was lovely inside, albeit tiny. It had originally been a chapel, and had then been used for storage by a farmer before being converted into a cosy home. The jumbly bare-stone gable walls tapered upwards into a vaulted roof space where a mezzanine had been built, connected by a wooden stairway to the open-plan living area. There was a small bathroom to the left of the front door, complete with a hot water shower, and there were two electric heaters downstairs. Everything looked clean and pleasant, and the only sound I could hear through the foot-thick walls was the faint mooing and baaing of my prospective neighbours. I couldn't have asked for a more perfect setting in which to write. Well, a Wi-Fi signal would have been the cherry on top. But surprisingly there was a strong mobile signal in the area, so I was able to use my phone to get online. I agreed to move in right away.

I stayed in 'Bethlehem Barn', as it was called, for four months over the winter of 2016/17, and I wrote the lion's share of *Mindfulness and the Big Questions* there. Despite the intense snowy cold outside, the heaters kept me snug and warm inside, especially at night, the hot air nestling in the eaves like an extra duvet. The barn had been advertised as a holiday cottage, and I don't think the owners expected to have any tenants at this time of year, so I got a good deal on the rent – £400 per month, all bills included. I lived off my savings for the first few months, and after that my parents generously helped me out with a cash transfusion. Though I was working extremely hard on the book, I soon settled into a delightful routine. If I got bored or mentally tired, I went for walks in the surrounding countryside – up hills, down dales, along former railway tracks, and beside the banks of the serene River Tees. If I got hungry, I popped into Middleton-in-Teesdale (a large village) or Barnard Castle (a nearby town), to get some food. And if I got lonely, I chatted to the staff of the various local cafes and pubs. Everyone was friendly and welcoming, despite their evident bemusement at the sudden presence of a scruffy cockney philosopher in their sleepy part of the world.

Only the sheep seemed indifferent. Grazing their way right up to the exterior of the barn, they must have seen many a holidaymaker come and go. I tried to make friends with these stoical fleecy natives, but they weren't interested. In fact, their incredible nonchalance occasioned a fun game I started playing whenever I got bored. I would go outside and say something silly, usually in a silly voice, in the general direction of the sheep. Sometimes they would pay me no attention, their heads down, chomping on grass as though they'd heard it all before. But other times a few of them would look up, with a quizzical expression on their faces. What were they thinking? Why had they looked up when I'd sung "empty chairs at empty tables" but not when I'd shouted "wolf"? I never worked it out; sheep psychology is not my thing. Nevertheless, I enjoyed the challenge of seeing how many sheep I could get to look up at me in one go. On a couple of occasions, I achieved a full house – a 100% response rate, a rare pleasure. Orwell was right when he said that writers need space. He was also right when he said that writers are attention seekers.

Sadly, my time in the barn had to end: the owners had already (before I came onto the scene) accepted a booking for late February. For the next couple of weeks, I stayed in another holiday cottage, in Middleton-in-Teesdale, but the rent was twice as expensive, and I felt guilty having once again asked my parents for more money. I didn't want to keep sponging off them... but the book wasn't finished, and the deadline was looming. My stress levels were rising, and my focus was faltering. I figured that the best option was to ask my parents if I could move back home for a while, while I finished the book. They agreed, being accommodating as ever (literally). So I bundled my stuff back into my car, said a sad farewell to the Durham Dales (including the sheep, all of whom ignored me), and sped down the motorway towards London.

I should have known better. In all the years that I've struggled to find and afford a decent place to live, there have been many occasions when I haven't exactly covered myself in glory. However, the next few months of my life were the most inglorious of all. I relate what happened with a sense of guilt and disquiet, but these experiences were part of my own personal housing crisis, and therefore they belong in this book.

I fell out with my parents after a single night back home. I must admit I had a sinking feeling as soon as I walked through the front door. I suddenly realised that my splendid isolation was well and truly over; now I was very much getatable. It wasn't so much my physical proximity to my parents that unsettled me, but, rather, being in their mental orbit again. Fundamentally, their attitude hadn't changed over the years; they disapproved of my chosen career and lifestyle. For as long as I can remember, almost every time I have interacted with my parents they have tried, subtly or not-so-subtly, to persuade me to get a 'proper' job. This time round, it was no different. Sitting in the lounge with them, I found myself once again trying to justify my choices and, well, my hopes. But to no avail. My hopes were not my parents' hopes.

This shouldn't have mattered to me as much as it did. But I was ragged from working so hard for so long, the stratum of my self-control hardened but brittle. The harder you've worked on something, the harder it is to hear that you've been on the wrong track. What haunts me is that maybe my dad was right; maybe I am unlikely ever to make a living as a writer. Maybe, as the discussion lurched into a row, I protested too much, in the Shakespearian sense. Certainly I felt guiltier than usual, having lived off my parents' money in the preceding months. But the guiltier I felt about disappointing my parents, the angrier I felt about their disappointment. Our mutual ill-feeling was like a genie let out of a bottle, and the genie was a specialist in imprecations. Like a typhoon, the row went around in circles, widening and intensifying as it rose, picking up debris, remnants of the past, stuff that is too painful for me to write about. The atmosphere became apocalyptic. I left home hurriedly, on very bad terms with my parents.

I didn't know where to go next. All I knew was that I had to finish my book. Driven by second nature, I headed up the motorway towards Cambridge. I knew someone there who I hoped would help me: the widow of a late friend of mine. My friend had been an elderly man when I met him, a few years previously, through the Cambridge Conservative Association. I had turned up to a few of their meetings hoping to talk to some interesting new people, and he and I soon became friends. We enjoyed many stimulating discussions about politics and life, until, tragically, he died of cancer in 2014. I stayed in touch with his widow, and after I left my parents' house in the spring of 2017 I phoned her to tell her I had nowhere to go. She kindly invited me to stay; "any friend of my husband's is a friend of mine" she said. I will always be grateful to her for her being a Good Samaritan.

After a few days at her house, I felt a little better, and I started looking for a job and a new place to live in Cambridge. Soon enough I found a new delivery job – six evenings a week at another Indian takeaway. But finding a room wasn't so straightforward. I checked out a few rooms, but they were affordable for the usual reasons. I feared that I would struggle to finish my book if I was surrounded by noise and madness again. I wondered whether the alternative was staring me in the face. I knew that my late friend and his wife had had numerous lodgers in the past; indeed, these lodgers had stayed in the room that I was sleeping in. And I knew that they had all been young people connected in some way to the university. Maybe I would be a suitable candidate. I decided to ask my friend's widow if, by any chance, she was looking for another lodger; perhaps she would let me stay until I finished my book. Of course, I suspected deep down that she wasn't looking for another lodger – otherwise presumably she would have asked me. By asking her, I was imposing on her for a second time. Yet, once again, she kindly assented. She suggested an extremely low rent of £100 per month; I insisted on doubling it, which was still less than half the going rate. And so it was that I found myself living with another live-in landlady, in another beautiful big house, this time in the most desirable part of Cambridge.

For a while, my new landlady and I rubbed along fine. I didn't want to get under her feet, so in the daytimes I mostly wrote in cafes and the University Library. And at night we didn't disturb each other: the house had three floors, with my bedroom being on the ground floor and hers on the top floor. She was a night owl, so in the evenings she was usually awake when I got home from work; she would call out hello, and I would go upstairs to the living area on the first floor and sit with her in front of the TV. When we weren't watching anything in particular we would chat happily. Like her late husband, she loved to talk about politics. Mercifully, she shared his general political outlook, so I wasn't subjected to any angry lefty sloganeering.

To be honest, I must have been an absolute nightmare to be around at that time: a manic, nail-biting, twitching bundle of nerves. My nervousness was partly due to creative energy, but also due to anxiety. Over a long period of time, my sense of autonomy had been eroded – by the disapproval of my parents, by the rows with my friends, by the aggravations at work, and by the housing crisis with all its ramifications for my life. Uncertainty is like a predator; when I looked in the mirror I hardly recognised myself, such was the hunted look on my face. I tried to talk to my landlady about my worries. She was a good listener – perhaps a little too good. She had been trained as a counsellor, in a method whereby the counsellor listens without ever comment-ing on what is said. I guess some people appreciate this approach; they don't want to be 'judged'. But not me. I needed advice – practical and emotional advice –

based on good judgement. When I talked to my landlady about my worries I felt as though I was baying at the moon.

Strangely – or perhaps it's not so strange when you think about it – my landlady's penchant for impassive listening had a flipside: she also had a penchant for telling long, rambling stories. Some of these stories lasted for half an hour or more. I was desperate not to appear ungrateful, so I always sat and listened politely. In the evenings this could be a real chore, especially if I was tired after a busy shift at work. Concentrating on the road for six hours straight, trying not to plough into mobile-phone-toting pedestrians or earphone-wearing cyclists or abject drivers, was mentally exhausting; the last thing I needed was to have my mental focus tested again when I arrived home. Keeping track of all the antics of all the protagonists in my landlady's tortuous stories made me feel as though I had taken some sort of autism-inducing drug. Still, she had done me a huge favour in letting me stay; the least I could do was nod and smile.

My landlady's background was unconventional. She was exceedingly rich, having inherited a fortune, some of which she had invested in property. Her wealth had enabled her to live a life not unlike mine; she had done some writing, editing and teaching but she had never had a 'proper' career. At one stage she had even worked as a postwoman. She was a wanderer, her overriding interest being religion; but not just any religion: *all* religions. She was what you might call an ecumenical believer in God. Over the years, she had lived in various cloistered religious communities, always trying to find the true path to salvation but at the same time knowing that the object of her devotion must remain elusive: a self-declared 'mystic', she had studied deeply in the mystical traditions of Christianity, Islam and Buddhism. Personally, I find mysticism interesting, especially in the Buddhist tradition. Does the universe have a mysterious hidden source that can bring meaning and solace to our lives? It's a question worth asking, even though I suspect the answer is no. I believe that the universe exists, and we're in it, and we're conscious of being in it, and we're free, which enables us to live meaningfully and to strive to be good... but there's no more to human existence than human existence. Our lives are what they are, nothing more, nothing less.

I thought I was on safe ground telling my landlady that I was an atheist and an existentialist. After all, I figured that if God is elusive there's not much involved in believing in him. A mystical God, it seems to me, is like the active ingredient in a homeopathic remedy: non-existent to all practical purposes. But I misjudged the strength of my landlady's religious conviction. To her, God's elusiveness points to the opposite conclusion: if we can't grasp God beyond the world, we'll have to consider the world itself as godly. The whole of reality, on this view, becomes a manifestation of God; reality itself becomes other-worldly, an illusion, shimmering like the surface of a deep ocean. Far from being insignificant, God's elusiveness becomes all-encompassing; there is nothing except God.

This might sound pointlessly abstract, but unfortunately my landlady's religious devotion lurked – Godlike – beneath every conversation we had. It was only a matter of time before the topic of religion came bobbing awkwardly to the surface. When it did, I remember blithely announcing that I don't believe in God. And I remember my landlady's response, beginning with the look on her face, as though a pall of dark clouds had swept over her features. The soft lines of happiness in the corners of her eyes became sharp streaks of anxiety. Her gentle sunny brow became a wintry field, harshly furrowed. "Why don't you believe in God?" she asked. I was taken aback by the severity of her tone, so I apologetically muttered something about the suffering of life; even if God exists, he doesn't deserve to be worshipped, I ventured. "That's your decision," she said, closing down the conversation; 'God exists' and 'God is good' are the non-negotiable slogans of theists, I suppose. I made a mental note not to raise the topic of God again.

But we kept clashing over religion, perhaps inevitably. Actually, the next time we clashed I can only say that I *suspect* religion was the source of our disagreement. We were discussing conservatism, when the topic of gay marriage came up. I am a supporter of gay marriage. There is evidence to suggest that marriage makes people happier and healthier, and I don't see why gay people should be excluded from these benefits. Some people argue that allowing homosexuals to marry undermines the role of marriage in keeping families together. But I don't buy that argument. Plenty of married heterosexual couples don't rear children. And just because marriage helps heterosexual couples stay together for the sake of their kids, this doesn't mean marriage should be restricted to heterosexuals; are we going to deprive homosexuals of *anything* that helps heterosexual couples stay together? Romantic breaks? Separate toothbrushes? Mutual friends? However, there are many conservatives who disagree with me on this. Because I agree with conservatives about so much else, I'm always interested to hear their arguments against gay marriage.

My landlady offered an interesting argument that I hadn't heard before. She insisted that the word marriage simply *means* a union between a man and a woman. The attempt to include homosexual marriage within the concept of marriage is, on this view, an act of Orwellian newspeak; like calling war peace, or slavery freedom. If valid, this argument could explain why some conservatives are so ardently opposed to gay marriage. The attempt to force people to believe impossible things is the hallmark of totalitarianism, and the opposition to totalitarianism is the hallmark of conservatism. Opposing gay marriage would, accordingly, become a laudable political act. Of course, there's another explanation for why some conservatives disapprove of gay marriage: many conservatives are religious, and many religious people think homosexuality is a sin. Many religious people oppose gay marriage because they construe marriage as a divinely sanctioned institution, its meaning set in stone for all eternity by God himself.

I didn't ask my landlady if she thought marriage takes its meaning from God; I was too scared to mention God again. But as the conversation progressed I suddenly recognised on her face the same pall of disapproval that I had seen when I told her I was an atheist. She proceeded to resist all my efforts to argue that marriage doesn't necessarily mean heterosexual marriage. I pointed out, for instance, that the word marriage originally meant 'joined together' – in this sense, any two entities can be 'married' – in which case there is no reason homosexuals can't be married. No, she said, marriage in human relationships means heterosexual marriage. I also pointed out that sometimes words change their meanings without the process being gerrymandered in a totalitarian way; the word 'atom', for instance, originally meant 'unsplittable' but now we know that atoms are very much splittable, and we still use the same word. Perhaps, I suggested, the discovery that gay marriage is morally acceptable could likewise be counted as progress in human understanding. No, she said, you cannot discover that marriage means something other than what it really means. We had reached a kind of stand-off, the conversation suddenly undergoing a subtle but perceptible shift. A friend of mine once employed a marvellous metaphor to describe this kind of shift: it is an 'event horizon'. In physics, an event horizon is the point at which an object cannot escape from a black hole because the gravitational pull being exerted on the object is overwhelmingly strong. Similarly, when a conversation reaches an event horizon, neither participant can escape from an overpowering sense of mutual frustration; the debate inevitably becomes repetitive, going round in circles, spiralling into an acrimonious ending. The important thing, my friend said, is to see the event horizon coming before you cross it – to go into reverse before the point of no return is reached. Unfortunately, my landlady and I sailed enthusiastically across the event horizon when we discussed gay marriage. We became locked into a pedantic row that carried on into the early hours, and we both went to bed feeling aggrieved.

That should have been the end of it. Certainly, the next morning I sensed that both myself and my landlady were making a special effort to be cheery and polite to each other. But I knew I had annoyed her. And, worse, I suddenly felt as though I was getting in her way, getting under her feet. I already knew I was imposing upon her; but now I *felt* it too. As much as I needed my space to live, she obviously needed hers; but she was far too decent a person to admit it.

Or so I thought. In fact, we were speeding towards the mother of all black holes.

We crossed the event horizon a few days after I had finished the manuscript for *Mindfulness and the Big Questions*. Perhaps there were subconscious reasons for this uncanny timing, on both sides; who knows. One evening, I came home from work, as usual, listened to my landlady tell a few long stories, as usual, and the conversation turned to conservatism, as usual. We started talking about how the welfare state promotes irresponsible behaviour. I made a disapproving remark about parents who conceive a child without making adequate preparations – financial, practical and emotional arrangements – for the future welfare of the child. There are few greater sins in my opinion. My landlady agreed with me – up to a point. She agreed that state welfare encourages bad behaviour. But she thought I had gone too far in my opprobrium for irresponsible people, including irresponsible parents.

"Don't forget, Ben," she said, "that every act is an act of love."

This was another intriguing argument that I hadn't heard before. If true, it could mitigate all manner of sins on the part of misbehaving people. I asked my landlady to explain what she meant.

"Every act is, deep down, an act of love because the

whole universe is an act of love. Everything is made out of love," she said.

Oh no – God again.

I was mindful that an event horizon might be looming. I was determined not to cause a row. But my landlady's confident statement was too preposterous to ignore, not to mention too interesting. Everything is made out of love? I started probing the notion, gently, abstractly, at first.

"How can love create a universe?" I asked.

"Nothing is more powerful than love."

"But why does love exist rather than nothing?"

"Because love is the reason for everything."

"So why is there so much suffering, if everything is made out of love?"

"Because sometimes love goes wrong."

"Is cancer an act of love?"

"Love is mysterious."

"What about mundane activities like going to the toilet? When I go to the toilet is that an act of love?"

"Yes, you go to the toilet because you love the feeling of not needing to go to the toilet anymore."

"OK, what about evil acts? What about the Moors Murders? Were they acts of love?"

"I'm not going to answer that question."

(Event horizon.)

"Why not?"

"Because I know what you're doing."

"What I am doing?"

"You're trying to pin me."

"No, I'm not. I'm asking you a 'yes or no' question."

"I'm not going to answer it."

"Why not? If everything is made out of love, then

the Moors Murders must have been acts of love. Do you think they were?"

"YOU HORRIBLE LITTLE BASTARD, GET OUT OF MY HOUSE!"

No, I didn't see that coming either. Love is indeed mysterious! I guess I should have backed down instantly and apologised, for my own good as well as my landlady's. But a feeling of injustice stung my insides. I was being vilified for nothing other than pointing out the logical implications of my landlady's own belief. As she glared at me, with a look of wounded fury in her eyes, she didn't look much like a person who genuinely believed that the universe is the handwork of a benevolent God. She looked like a terrified cat with its claws out.

I've always suspected that theists, with their claim that there is benevolence in everything, are in fact reacting pathologically to their own sense of persecution. After all, if the universe has a hidden supernatural creator, then human beings are, at least temporarily, in a sort of prison; that is, we are in a place from which we require 'salvation'. Moreover, in this prison, we are at risk of terrible suffering inflicted by our creator. We are at his mercy, because only he can protect us, or save us, from his own creation. No wonder, then, that theists prostrate themselves so utterly at the feet of their tormentor. They are inflamed by a sort of cosmological Stockholm Syndrome; they perceive God to be such a threat, and so powerful, that the safest course of action is to empathise with him unconditionally; they fall in love with him, seeing him as someone who is worthy of their love because he loves them back. Accordingly, anyone who challenges the validity of this loving relationship poses a threat to the welfare of theists; if they were to stop loving their captor, they would displease him, which would place them in even graver danger than that which attracted them to God in the first place. The more deeply you probe theism, the more ardently you will be resisted. The more rigorously you point out that God – if he even exists – deserves to be hated and feared, the more fiercely theists will profess their love for God. In my view, theists and other religious believers suffer from a religious version of philosophical hypochondria. They neurotically and needlessly make a problem out of life itself; they try to flee from their existence, perversely seeking refuge in the hidden source of their existence, and, in the process, they claim to possess special insight that is beyond worldly criticism.

I feel bad about what happened with my landlady, but as she sat there, her soul blaring at me, her words of fury hanging in the air like a cry of existential rage, she morphed – in my eyes – from a Good Samaritan into the kind of self-styled benevolent overlord that I had come to resent. She was God's servant, but she was also his emissary. In effect she was saying: to experience benevolence you must accept subjugation. I couldn't accept this – not just philosophically, but in mundane terms too. In my mind, at that moment, my plight as an atheist blurred into my plight as young person amid Britain's housing crisis. I felt hunted, but I didn't want to be offered shelter if being offered shelter meant sacrificing my psychological independence. I didn't want to be patronised – not in that sense. I didn't want to be tranquilised by the complacent shibboleths of a generation of hippies who had bought houses cheap then overseen a housing crisis for successive generations. I didn't want to conform to utopian nonsense, whether of the socialist or religious variety; I had no truck with the idea that we're all part of a loving community, on earth or in God; I didn't want to pay a price for other (wealthier) people's comforting illusions.

At any rate, that was how I felt; that was the thorn-bush of notions I had in my mind at that moment. I looked my landlady in the eye, and I said: "You're bullying me."

She replied: "You are a horrible little bastard and I don't want you in my house."

"I'll leave in the morning."

"I want you to leave now."

"I can't, it's too late. I'll leave in the morning, I promise."

And with that, my landlady stomped upstairs.

I woke early, before her. After I had packed my stuff into my car and cleaned my room, I went looking for my shoes. They weren't where I had left them, in the hallway. When I had first moved in, my landlady had gifted me a pair of shoes that had belonged to her late husband. I had worn them every day since. Now I couldn't find them anywhere. She must have crept downstairs and taken them away in the night. I drove away from Cambridge with my running trainers on my feet, and a feeling of implacable sadness in my heart.

15.

This time I knew I was leaving Cambridge for good. I had hung around this town for too long. The problem was, I had never completely given up on the idea of having an academic career, albeit an academic career on my terms. For a decade, I had failed to grow out of the mindset of being a newly-minted Doctor of Philosophy, trying to build an academic reputation before moving into a permanent role in a university, whether in Cambridge or elsewhere. I had been living in limbo.

And yet things might have turned out very differently for me in Cambridge. Back in 2009, a year after I had completed my PhD, I received a surprising email. The department where I studied is affiliated to a museum, and the email was from the museum's Curator. She had been a close friend of the Head of Department, Peter Lipton – my late supervisor. She wrote to tell me a staggering piece of news. The day Peter had died (the day after he had told me "there should be funding for someone like you"), he had bumped into the Curator in the corridor, and he had made a suggestion to her. For many years, they had colluded on an 'unofficial' scheme for helping certain students. Occasionally a PhD student would come along who, for one reason or another, needed a helping hand with developing an academic career. Usually this would be someone from a non-affluent background. Peter suggested to the Curator that I was a deserving candidate. He suggested – as per their unofficial scheme – that she should offer me a part-time research job in the museum, to allow me a period of time during which I could work on enhancing my academic CV. The Curator had concurred. But when Peter died, she was so overcome with grief, and disbelief, she forgot about his suggestion. A year later, she had contacted me to say she had suddenly remembered their conversation. By this time, however, I had already moved back to London, and I had temporarily given up on the idea of an academic career. I had set my heart on paying off my debts, sorting out my health problems, and becoming a popular writer. If I had known about Peter's suggestion immediately after I submitted my PhD, I would definitely have taken him up on it, and I might well be working as an academic now.

Oh well. I only have myself to blame; I could have accepted the Curator's job offer, even if it came later than intended. The irony is, I proceeded to spend much of the next decade trying to keep in touch with the academic world, in the hope of resurrecting my academic career. I wrote several articles that were published in academic journals, but the only journals that ever accepted my work were marginal. This was a problem for my career, because academia is currently dominated by a bureaucratic system in which the government attempts to assess the academic 'Impact' of each researcher's work. In each subject, there are a handful of journals that are deemed to have a 'high' impact, and if you want to get funding – most of which today comes from the government – you have to publish work in these journals. Unfortunately, when it comes to philosophy (and most other humanities subjects), the high-impact journals tend to publish boring, formulaic work – hence Professor Lipton's scepticism about my chances of ever receiving funding. Moreover, my chances of getting an article about philosophical hypochondria published in a high-impact philosophy journal were minuscule; the editors of these journals are avid philosophical hypochondriacs.

There are many perverse aspects to the current funding system in academia. For one thing, the idea that government bureaucrats are the most appropriate people to judge the quality of academic research is insane – straight out of the communist playbook. Only slightly less insane is the idea that academics should be judged on the *quantity* of their published work. This criterion tends to exclude researchers who are working on deep, slow-burning projects (not to mention researchers who don't publish much work during their lifetimes, a category that includes some of the most famous philosophers in history). The culture of 'publish or perish' in academia has led to a ludicrous situation in which churning out written work makes academics so busy that they rarely have time to read each other's publications; everyone's talking, no one's listening. Even more ridiculous is the fact that this system ensures that academics hardly have time to interact with their students. No wonder there is a mental health crisis among students on university campuses: mentoring – the imparting of wisdom – has become a relic. However, by far the most perverse aspect of this system is that when academics apply for funding, they not only have to demonstrate their 'research excellence' to the government, they also have to demonstrate that their work will have a 'social impact' – another idea straight out of the communist playbook. Academics are forced into explaining why the extremely abstract work they have published in high-impact journals is in fact vitally important to everyday folk. Sometimes these explanations may be valid, especially in scientific research. But often they are unavoidably convoluted and insincere, especially in the humanities. It's a system that injects sclerotic bogusness into the heart of the intelligentsia.

In turn, academia's modern obsession with 'social impact' has contributed to the rampant spread of political correctness on campuses. Government bureaucrats tend to favour academic work that fits in with their leftist, statist agenda. Accordingly, the bureaucrats' favourite research topics include 'climate change' (because climate change supposedly justifies a bigger role for the government in our lives), 'diversity' (because diversity supposedly requires government-imposed quotas and affirmative action in order to prevent racist, sexist and homophobic biases from dominating recruitment decisions), and 'poverty and inequality' (because poverty and inequality supposedly can only be reduced through government control). With the bureaucrats holding the purse strings, universities have become places where academics either enthusiastically champion leftist views or daren't challenge those views. Bizarrely, while university departments and student populations have themselves been transformed by measures to increase diversity, campuses have been subjected to an overall decline in the diversity of viewpoints.

This all became especially galling to me in the years after my PhD, because by that time most of the work I was doing in philosophy was literally having a positive impact on all kinds of people. The *Journal of Modern Wisdom* was being read and digested by thousands of people outside of academia. *Cycle Lifestyle* was full of commentary on topics such as well-being, freedom, responsibility, the common good, and caring for the local environment. My books were bringing philosophical ideas to a non-specialist readership, including tens of thousands of readers of *Einstein and the Art of Mindful Cycling*. I was writing numerous essays, articles and blogs for freely accessible, popular websites. And I was regularly presenting talks and seminars on my work to non-philosophers. Yet, bureaucratically speaking, it all counted for nothing. The bureaucrats I needed to impress were only interested in the bogus 'social impact' of work published in high-impact philosophy journals that are rarely read by anyone, including their contributing authors.

In an attempt to boost my publishing credentials, I approached scores of academic publishers with my idea for a book about philosophical hypochondria. I was met with scores of rejections. Many of the commissioning editors said that they didn't have a 'series' into which they could place my book – this was the same excuse that many of the commercial publishers had used too. Bizarrely, none of today's publishers seem to have thought of creating a series for original ideas. Or perhaps this is not so bizarre: people who try to categorise everything in advance have no room for creativity in their tedious schemes.

There was only one occasion when my book wasn't

rejected outright by an academic publisher. What followed was one of the craziest episodes of my life. The commissioning editor of this particular publisher had decided to send my book proposal (including a sample chapter) away to be 'peer reviewed'. This was an encouraging sign. Typically, peer review involves two suitable experts assessing a book proposal, and, if the feedback is positive, the publisher will proceed. I was asked to name a suitable reviewer – which is standard procedure – so I named an American professor who had written an article for the *Journal of Modern Wisdom*. I hoped she would be sympathetic to my ideas, and, indeed, she wrote an extremely positive review of my proposal. However, the other reviewer was selected by the publisher – which is, again, standard procedure. And the other reviewer didn't like my proposal. He or she – they were anonymous – seemed to think my ideas were rather backward. At one point, the reviewer compared me to a 'climate change denier'. This was a low blow, because the book I was proposing had nothing to do with climate change. However, in due course, the commissioning editor contacted me to tell me that, because of the negative review, she had decided not to publish my book. I replied by pointing out that the positive review was much more positive than the negative review was negative. The commissioning editor agreed. She also noted that she frequently published books on the basis of a single positive review. But on this occasion, she explained, she would have to decline "because of my treatment of climate change".

Eh? I replied by pointing out that my book wasn't about climate change; the reviewer had used the term 'climate change denier' by way of an analogy. The reviewer was not literally (and therefore was literally not) calling me a climate change denier. But the editor was insistent. She informed me that she had recently attended a meeting with her colleagues, including various colleagues at the university to which the publisher was affiliated, and everyone at the meeting had agreed that climate change was a serious issue; they had all agreed that the university's publishing arm ought to support this issue vigorously. As a result, she continued, the reviewer's comments about climate change were "a red flag"; she couldn't justify publishing a book that might cause controversy in this regard. Naturally, my next question was: "Are you joking?!" She might as well have rejected my book proposal because someone said I reminded them of a witch. (And even if I had been a climate change denier, should that have meant that my book about philosophy was beyond the pale? Or even if I had challenged climate change in my book, should such a book be beyond the pale?) Just like in local government, image was everything; I was wasting my time bringing reality into it.

My lack of academic publishing credentials explains why I've never bothered to apply for a job as an academic philosopher: I'd be wasting my time, like someone applying for a pilot's job without a pilot's licence. But I have applied for various other jobs in universities, including philosophy-related roles in administration, teaching, and outreach, and even a role as a writer in residence. I've been rejected every time, which is harder to understand. Meanwhile, my attempt to broaden my academic competence to include the study of well-being has also been unfruitful, career-wise. When I volunteered for the Well-being Institute in Cambridge, I worked very hard, setting up a series of open lectures for the public, and a series of interdisciplinary seminars for academics interested in the study of well-being. But none of this lead to gainful employment for me. I guess philosophers aren't supposed to broaden their horizons or attempt to broaden other people's horizons; philosophers are supposed to *pretend* that their work has an impact beyond philosophy, nothing more, nothing less.

There was one occasion when my work for the Well-being Institute led to a tangible opportunity for me. But the opportunity was swiftly snatched from my grasp. I had been invited by the Cambridge Medical School to present a series of seminars on well-being to stressed-out students during the examination period. The seminars weren't supposed to be academic – just informal discussion sessions to help the students. The organisers had read some of my work online and decided that I was a suitable person for the job. But before I accepted the offer, I thought I'd better consult the Director of the Well-being Institute. She wasn't impressed.

"Why did they approach you?" she asked.

"I suppose it's because I manage the mailing lists. The Medical School probably received an email from me at some point."

"But why didn't they ask me? I am Director of the Institute."

"I don't know, but I'd like to take them up on their offer."

"The problem is, Ben, I can think of hundreds of people who are more qualified than you to present these seminars."

"So can I. But those people weren't asked. I was."

"I'd like to talk to the person who contacted you."

"OK."

And that was the end of that; the Director of the Well-Being Institute appointed someone else to present the seminars at the Medical School. I resigned from my role soon afterwards. The truth is, the Director didn't like me, for ideological reasons. In her opinion, the responsibility for promoting well-being in society belongs to the government. (No doubt, this opinion was convenient for her when she was applying for academic funding.) In my opinion, however, the responsibility for promoting well-being in society belongs to cultural leaders, communities and non-governmental organisations; I'm a communitarian, a big believer in the Big Society. That's why I've been personally involved in entrepreneurial activities designed to promote well-being. Civil society, I believe, is self-creating: a bottom-up process, not a gift from self-styled benevolent overlords. Alas, when I confessed this heterodox view to the Director, she screwed up her face and said "hmmm, interesting", by which she meant that she wasn't in the slightest bit interested. As ever, my efforts to achieve academic credibility foundered on the rocks of statism.

So there was bitterness in my soul when I finally left Cambridge. Nothing had worked out for me there. Even my own department had let me down. At one stage, I applied to become an 'Honorary Associate' of the department – a nominal title which is sometimes bestowed on intellectuals who have done valuable work outside of academia. But my department declined give me the title. I wasn't surprised; their cold shouldering of my work was a continuation of a theme. Ten years ago, my doctoral research was considered so controversial in Cambridge that no one in my department or indeed the whole university was willing to examine my thesis. (I remember Professor Lipton informing me – with his characteristic wit – that most of the prospective examiners had come up with lame excuses like "I can't do it this month; I'm washing my hair".) Normally, PhD candidates are allocated an 'internal' examiner from within the university and an 'external' examiner from another university. But in an unusual move, I was allocated two external examiners – both of whom were from Durham University, and both of whom, it turned out, appreciated my work; in their respective examiner reports they described my PhD as "remarkable and original" and "bold and original". A few years after that, the philosophy department at Durham conferred the title of Honorary Associate on me; they even agreed that the *Journal of Modern Wisdom* could be officially 'affiliated' to the department. With all this in my mind, fifteen years after moving to Cambridge to start my PhD, I finally accepted the obvious. I knew which side my bread was buttered on. I finally did what I should have done ages ago: I moved back to the city of Durham. And this time I intended to stay.

After being thrown out of my landlady's house, my move North was swift and disorganised. I picked up the remainder of my possessions from the lock-up in Cambridge, crammed everything into my longsuffering car, which sagged under the load, and made my way gingerly up the A1. On the way I stopped at a service station and went online to search for a place to live. A cheap room in a house in a former pit village near Durham caught my eye. I called the landlady and we arranged to meet at the house in the evening.

A few hours later, I arrived at a council estate high on a windswept hill a few miles outside the city of Durham. The area was somewhat rundown, albeit with an amazing view over the rooftops and across the hills. As for the house, it was very rundown. It was filthy, with a layer of grime covering the floors and the kitchen surfaces. It stank of cigarette smoke. It was falling apart, with the carpets unravelling, the wall-paper peeling off, and many of the fixtures held in place by masking tape. Yet, strangely, I liked the house. It had a good atmosphere somehow. And the rent was only £240 per month, with no contract. I agreed to move in right away (not that I had much choice).

Fortunately, my new housemates turned out to be pleasant and quiet (albeit untidy). There were four of us altogether. In the downstairs bedroom was a chain-smoking Geordie chef. He was a jolly character, but I didn't see much of him, because he worked day and night in a pub kitchen. When he arrived home at midnight he didn't disturb anyone, because the rest of us slept upstairs. A few months after I moved in, he went on holiday to Thailand to see his "wife", and he never returned. His room remained empty, partly because its lingering tobacco stench put off prospective tenants.

The upstairs bedrooms, excluding mine, contained a Bulgarian man who worked in a factory, and a Chinese research engineer who worked at the university. Roughly the same age as me, they were both generous and cheerful characters; we soon became friends. The three of us would sit together in the living room, or in cafes and restaurants, joking and laughing and chatting freely about all manner of subjects. It was fascinating to hear the views of people who had grown up in such different circumstances to me. From my Chinese friend I learned a lot about today's communist government in China. He convinced me that Donald Trump's so-called 'trade war' against China is entirely justified as a response to the aggressive product dumping and copyright acquisition practices of the communists. Yet my Chinese friend, just like my Hong Kongese landlord in Cambridge, was a trenchant defender of communism, despite preferring to live in the UK where he was "freer" than he would be in China. In my friend's case, however, I felt I could explain this paradox. Over the last few decades, the Communist Party in China has freed up the economy without confessing that communism was a colossal error. Indeed, when my friend was at school he was taught that communism itself was responsible for the recent economic gains of China. This explains both my friend's dim view of capitalist democracies and some of his bizarre views on history. He once summarised the Second World War as "all the democracies fighting" and he insisted that "the difference between the Nazis and the Allies is like the difference between two football teams" – that is, there was no substantial difference between them. He also insisted that the hideous death toll in China under Mao was due to "natural disasters". Such nonsense could only be believed by someone who had been taught from a young age that China's recent economic successes were a triumph of communism, as opposed to a triumph of market liberalisation, the logical endpoint of which is democracy. To such a person, the superior freedom enjoyed by the British is an incidental feature of our society, not its defining characteristic.

My Bulgarian friend, having lived under Soviet rule during his childhood, was no friend of communism. He spoke scathingly of the "idiots" who wanted to restore communist rule in his homeland. For him, the worst aspect of communism was that it restricted people's movement. For this reason, he was a staunch supporter of the EU; he prized free movement above all. He and I had some fascinating discussions about the EU – discussions that were never bitter, despite our contrasting opinions. Each of us understood where the other was coming from. I understood my Bulgarian friend's reasons for supporting the EU, and I understood his sense of personal injustice; he was undoubtedly working very hard and making a positive contribution to the UK economy. And he understood why I voted Leave; he understood that British workers needed houses and services just as much as he needed work. Sadly, several months after we became friends he lost his job and returned to Bulgaria. The Bulgarian government runs a scheme whereby citizens who have been made redundant while working abroad receive £700 a month for six months upon returning home; my friend decided to take the money. I hope he comes back someday.

Soon after I returned to Durham I resumed work as a delivery driver in the evenings, for various restaurants. The job has come with the usual ups and downs. Driving around in the hills, with the fresh, crisp, northern air whirling through the open window, has been wonderful for my state of mind and my creativity. Lucidity can be breathed in, I am tempted to say. But the job has also had demoralising aspects. As ever, I have had to deliver food to some grim council dwellings, their front gardens strewn with rusted kitchen appliances, old mattresses, children's toys, empty beer bottles, and piles of dog poo. Many of our customers are shockingly fat; some are drunk or on drugs; a few are aggressive. Their dogs are even scarier.

And, as ever, I have encountered some testy characters among my colleagues. In one restaurant, I worked with a 24-year-old Romanian man (he was the sous-chef) and his 17-year-old girlfriend, a local girl (she worked behind the counter). The Romanian had migrated to England to escape from the police in his homeland, where he had a history of "crashing cars and fighting", as he put it. Unfortunately, although he no longer owned a car, he was still fond of fighting, and he had found no shortage of opportunities to do so in England, much to the consternation of his girlfriend. Not long before I started in the job, she had fallen pregnant. He wasn't sure that the baby was his. The pair of them were living in a small house with the girl's mother; she – the mother – had recently left her husband, an alcoholic, and had already found a new partner. The whole setup was a recipe for stress for all concerned – stress that often spilled over into a tetchy atmosphere at the restaurant. The Romanian chef was constantly on the brink of leaving his girlfriend. When it was quiet at work he would come and stand beside the open window of my car and talk to me about his problems. I tried to help him, mostly by persuading him to help himself. He could start, I suggested, by not splurging his wages on cigarettes, beer and gambling, as he was accustomed to doing. If he spent his money more wisely he could afford to rent his own house, to provide a calm environment for his girlfriend and the forthcoming baby. These suggestions seemed to strike him with the force of a revelation. For my part, I was struck by the fact that, underneath all his bad choices, he was a likeable and hardworking young man.

There is a certain amount of poverty and crime in the North East, much of the poverty self-inflicted, and much of the crime inflicted by the self-inflicters on other poor people. But despite the region's patchy social problems, there is much to admire about its culture. For one thing, the pace of life is slower here than it is down south. The low pressure on housing makes life less frenzied for everyone. Moreover, the natives are, on the whole, steeped in old-fashioned 'common sense' values, such as stoicism, forthrightness, a willingness to poke fun at themselves and each other, hard work, practicality, trust, family loyalty, and community-spiritedness. These values are, I suppose, a legacy of the region's history of mining. The North East's miners were hardy souls who pulled their weight individually and stuck together in hard times. Almost every neighbourhood in the region retains a Working Men's Club, where the local people still congregate routinely. Most people round here are instinctively friendly; strangers will chat to you at any opportunity. There is, admittedly, a somewhat macho vibe in the air, which at first sight doesn't seem to tally with the evident friendliness and kindness of the menfolk as well as the womenfolk. But there is no paradox in this: tough people are polite, generous and non-confrontational because they don't want to rile each other. A 'live and let live' spirit prevails in the North East: a sense of respect and mutual tolerance that exemplifies the best in British culture.

Of course, politically the region has a longstanding tradition of left-wing representation. Yet you hear surprisingly little from the locals about Thatcher closing the mines. (And by no means were all the miners left-wing in the first place). Most people round here eschew the obsessive ideological socialism of *bien pensant* metropolitan types from the South of England (although the same can't be said for the university-educated local youngsters who have flocked to London in droves). The North East remains a 'Blue Labour' stronghold. Blue Labour supporters champion the free market, freedom of speech, and personal responsibility, while also emphasising social solidarity, particularly at the local level. In turn, Blue Labour supporters are wary of the impact of mass immigration on established communities, and wary of centralised government, including that of the EU. Personally, I think everyone on the left is far too nonchalant about the damage that the welfare state inflicts upon society, and far too flippant about the tendency of high taxation to lead to stifling bureaucracy, but the 'Blue' in the North East's version of Labour shows that a little conservatism goes a long way.

The native culture of the North East has had an impact on the atmosphere at Durham University. Compared to most universities, Durham hasn't succumbed quite so abjectly to the strictures of political correctness. Partly this is due to the preponderance of privately educated students in the university. But there is another factor, I suspect: the osmotic influence of the relaxed, tolerant, frank, non-confrontational culture of the locals. Durham University remains, for the time being, a place where free speech and political heterodoxy have a foothold.

Within a few months of my arrival, I contacted the philosophy department to tell them that I was back in town. Without hesitation they bestowed the new title of 'Honorary Fellow' on me – a title that gives me the status of a lecturer within the university albeit without the salary. This honour, I felt, was a vindication both of my work over the last decade and my decision to return to the North East.

Still, I am under no illusions about my chances of making a full return to academia (or the wisdom of doing so). Even in Durham University, political correctness is a force to be reckoned with. Recently I went for a coffee with one of the university's philosophy professors. Within minutes of our meeting up, he was effing and blinding about Donald Trump and Brexit: "I hope someone fucking murders Trump," he declared, adding that anyone who voted for Trump or Brexit is a "narrow-minded racist wanker". I was shocked to witness such an intelligent and influential man throwing a tantrum like an overgrown toddler. I was even more shocked that he automatically assumed I would agree with him. In some quarters, hatred of conservatism has become a sort of social glue that has replaced good manners. Nor has Durham University been immune to the bureaucratic control-freakery that has blighted academia in the last few decades. If I wanted to get an academic job, I'd still have to produce reams of bogusly impactful scholarly work; I'd have to toe the line – a randomly drawn line – like a driver pulled over and assessed for his psychological fitness by a bored police officer. Most likely – through a combination of choice and exigency – I'll continue operating on the intellectual black market.

But life in Durham has been good for me. After six months here, I decided to put down roots. I bought a house in the same former pit village that I've lived in since I first arrived. Owning my own home has been a delight. Jean-Paul Sartre may have exaggerated when he said that 'Hell is other people', but he wasn't exaggerating when he observed how powerfully people can be affected by *absences*, including the absence of other people. The absence of noise and disturbance, especially of late-night phone conversations; the absence of other people's mess; the absence of other people nagging me about my own mess; the absence of other people's political or religious views being rammed down my throat: living on my own has been a bonanza of absences for me, a gift for my creative spirit. The road here has been long, and there have been casualties, but now I am one of the lucky ones.

Perhaps you're wondering how I came to be able to afford to buy a house – even a house that cost less than £40,000. I'm still working deliveries most nights each week. I'm still a struggling writer, and maybe I always will be. Let's just say that the financing of my house purchase was a family affair, involving an inheritance from my late Grandma and a contribution from my parents. The details – as I have intimated already – are too painful for me to write about. Nothing is ever simple, especially when you are a non-socialist in a big family in which socialist views are the norm. Where I grew up, there was a saying that you shouldn't air dirty laundry in public. I haven't forgotten where I came from. And goodness knows I've already aired enough dirty laundry in this book. Now is a time for conclusions, for moving on – or, perhaps I should say, for staying in the same place for a while.

16.

The dictionary defines a 'perfect storm' as 'an especially bad situation caused by a combination of unfavourable circumstances'. The housing crisis fits this definition.

Only the most sanguine or ignorant person could deny that the lack of housing in the UK comprises an 'especially bad situation'. If any other vital resource – say, food or water – were in such short supply, a national emergency would have been declared by now. The statistics on housing are frightening. Since the 2008 financial crash, house prices have resumed their precipitous rise while outpacing earnings; at the time of writing, the average UK home costs in excess of £230,000. The cost of renting has soared too – to the highest level in Europe, with the average rent now at £750 per household per month, almost twice the European average of £400. The average Briton spends over 40% of his regular income on housing, a figure which is the third highest in Europe. One in seven private tenants pays over half his regular income on rent. The average first-time buyer pays a colossal £52,900 in rent before owning a home. Young people today are paying three times more for housing than their grandparents did. Escalating housing costs have been a major driver of inequality in the UK.

The housing crisis has scarred the social and physical landscape of Britain. Recent statistics have revealed over four and a half million people receiving housing benefits (including around a million people in work) at an annual cost of £24 billion to the government, while over a million families are currently on housing waiting lists in England alone. One report found that 24% of private renters in England had moved home in the past 12 months, and 29% had moved *three or more times in the past five years*. Our local areas have seen upheaval too: we have lost pubs, petrol stations, libraries, community centres, playing fields, and high street shops, with land usage skewed by house price rises. Moreover, the UK's newly built homes are among the smallest in Europe. Space-saving apartment blocks have sprung up like mushrooms in towns and cities, even though flats are not the homes most people ideally want to live in. One survey found that 50% of respondents wanted to live in a detached house, 22% in a bungalow, 2% in a low-rise flat, and 1% in a high-rise block. Developers know that affordability overrides all other considerations. For the same reason, aesthetic beauty has also become a pointless expense on the part of developers; such is the desperation of homebuyers, whatever is built will sell, no matter how ugly it is. In so many ways, the housing crisis has impoverished Britain.

As well as being an 'especially bad situation', the housing crisis fits the definition of a perfect storm insofar as the crisis was 'caused by a combination of unfavourable circumstances'. I have already discussed the most obvious of these circumstances: mass immigration, which has turned the UK into one of the top ten most congested countries in the world. In order to keep pace with the enormous increase in net migration that occurred during the last 20 years, we would have needed to build the equivalent of 20 new cities. In fact, not only did we fail to build these cities, the rate of housebuilding has declined steadily since the early 1970s (albeit with a small uptick in the last few years). The overall decline is another circumstance that has contributed to the crisis: the more the population has grown, the more sluggishly we have built homes; indeed, both the government and the private sector have slowed their rate of housebuilding. Sluggish development and mass immigration together have acted like a pincer on affordability. One of the fundamental laws of economics, the law of 'supply and demand', describes how prices rise in conditions of low supply and high demand. In these conditions, sellers can attract high prices because buyers, who are desperate to acquire the goods that are in short supply, bid each other up.

However, there's more to the story than this. In normal economic circumstances, high prices act as a signal – a source of information. They encourage businesses to produce more of the goods that are expensive; businesses, after all, want to get the largest possible returns. To the untrained ear, this might sound like a recipe for greed. But, actually, by stimulating an increase in the production of expensive goods, high prices ultimately benefit low earners. As more of the expensive goods are produced, their supply increases and their price drops. In other words, high prices inform the market that there is an unmet demand for specific goods, and, over time, the market diligently fulfils that demand. As money flows around the system, more and more people get what they want, even though the system as a whole is unplanned. In Adam Smith's famous phrase, the economy is like an 'invisible hand' that continually moves goods around to wherever they are needed most.

The invisible hand ought to have pegged back house prices even during an era of mass immigration. As prices rose, private developers ought to have rushed in eagerly to produce more houses, thus driving house prices down, or at least keeping them under control. In theory, 20 new cities ought to have been built. Another force that ought to have driven prices down is competition between private developers. Those who could produce houses more cheaply and efficiently than their competitors, perhaps by using innovative building methods, could have attracted customers by slashing prices. And yet, house prices rose and rose. Evidently, other 'unfavourable circumstances' intervened to disrupt the market's arc towards affordability.

Many of these circumstances were the result of the government's strict 'planning system' for housing. This planning system originated in the aftermath of the Second World War, when socialism was riding a tide of popularity in Britain. The defeat of the Nazis required a massive collective effort on the part of the British populace, an effort coordinated by the government. The success of this statist approach in wartime suggested to many people that a similar approach could work in peacetime too. Immediately after the war, the Conservative Prime Minister Winston Churchill was ousted in a landslide electoral victory for the Labour Party. The public, despite being on the winning side in a war against tyranny, had voted for a large reduction in their own freedom. The ensuing years saw the implementation of a raft of socialist policies, including a massive enlargement of the welfare state in 1945, the founding of the NHS in 1948, and, in between, the passing of new housing legislation. The Town and Country Planning Act of 1947 nationalised the planning system for new buildings, so that landowners who wanted to build on private land now needed permission from the government. In effect, the government was given – and still has – the last word on the amount and type of housing built in the UK.

One of the earliest challenges for the post-war government was to redress the housing shortage that had been caused by the Nazi bombardment of Britain's towns and cities. Hundreds of thousands of 'prefabricated' houses were erected in the immediate aftermath of the War. Prefabs were cheap, fairly flimsy structures, and few remain today, but they were much loved. In the 1950s and 1960s, the rate of government housebuilding remained high, and millions of permanent dwellings were constructed. This largescale project was accompanied by a policy known as 'slum clearance'. Almost a million houses – including lots of rows of Victorian terraces – were deemed inadequate by the government and destroyed, their inhabitants forcibly transferred into newly built modern dwellings. One in four of these new dwellings were situated in high-rise tower blocks. Mass-produced, identical living units were not only cheap; they appealed to the egalitarian ideals of the socialists.

However, despite these initial flurries of government housebuilding, the impact of the 1947 Act was negative. For a start, the policy of slum clearance was rash. Regardless of the immorality and questionable

wisdom of forcing 2.5 million people to move home –
thus driving apart extended families and established
communities – the destruction of so many houses
seems foolish in hindsight, given the desirability of
older housing stock today. Doubtless, some of the
streets that were cleared were grim. But, equally
doubtless, many perfectly decent homes were
bulldozed. Nor has hindsight been kind to the homes
that were built by the government during this period.
Most of the houses were pokey, ugly little dwellings.
And the high-rise flats that sprang up in the 1960s
were aesthetic and functional abominations that
became ridden with theft, vandalism, violence, drugs
and prostitution, not to mention human excrement.
Many were subsequently demolished by the government itself.

Hence, the post-war surge in government housebuilding has to be offset against the number of poor-
quality homes built and the number of good-quality
homes destroyed in the process. Nor, indeed, can this
surge be considered effective from a supply point of
view; large tower blocks were increasingly favoured
precisely because the government was failing to build
enough homes. By the early 1990s the number of
homes built annually by the government had fallen
from hundreds of thousands to a mere trickle. This
trickle continued into the new millennium and beyond,
despite the colossal rise in public spending that
occurred under New Labour in the 1990s – a rise
which suggests that the slump in government
housebuilding was caused by something other than
budgetary considerations.

One reason for the slump is that governments are
rarely as productive as free markets. Bureaucrats can

impress their political paymasters without ever leaving the office; strategy reports and spreadsheets and bogus statistics come to predominate over actual results. Moreover, since people's jobs are more secure in the public sector than in the private sector, failure in the former is tolerated more readily than in the latter; money comes easier in the public sector. Sometimes, of course, governments set themselves productivity 'targets'. But, even assuming that they're met, these targets are a double-edged sword. They can end up hampering productivity, because bureaucrats are not incentivised to exceed their targets – quite the opposite, because the targets represent ideal outcomes. In this way, targets become limits, as in the old anti-communist joke: "Why can't you get a tram in Krakow on a Friday? Because the tram-drivers will have fulfilled their production norm for the week by Thursday." In general, governments are less flexible than businesses. Unlike businesses, which can respond rapidly to changing market conditions – by increasing or decreasing their output accordingly – governments respond sclerotically, hampered by rigid decision-making structures and by a lack of on-the-ground information.

Since the Town and Country Planning Act was passed, the government's land development system has generally been organised into five-year planning blocks (a practice Stalin himself would no doubt have approved of). These planning blocks, whether applicable at the national or local level, have included overall targets for all new housing. Thus, all developers – whether public or private – have been thwarted by targets-cum-limits. Moreover, all developers have been thwarted by a large increase in planning regulations, the system having become increasingly complicated and difficult to navigate. In such a system, private developers are like sane men forced to wear straightjackets.

One planning policy has been particularly antagonistic to housebuilding by both the government and the private sector: the creation of 'green belts' in 1947. Located in the countryside around towns and cities, green belts are zones in which building is heavily limited, the goal being to reduce urban sprawl. The problem is, this goal has clashed with the UK's long-term trend for urban population growth. From within the UK and without, people have tended to migrate to where the jobs are – namely, cities. As a result, green belts have contributed to the spread of high-rise apartment blocks; for urban developers, the only way is up. And, worse, green belts have limited the supply of homes in precisely the areas where demand for homes is greatest.

In 1968, the Town and Country Planning Act was amended to try to make the green belt system more 'democratic'. Individuals and communities in rural areas were given the right to oppose new housing developments. But, despite its intentions, this amendment further restricted housing supply in Britain. The complaints of existing property owners have often delayed new developments, or vetoed them altogether, the latter outcome made more likely by the fact that local councillors have often been asked to adjudicate on contentious cases; naturally, elected councillors have tended to support existing homeowners. Indeed, by the time of the 1997 general election, rural homeowners had become so electorally powerful that both New Labour and the Conservatives campaigned on a platform of prioritising the development of 'brownfield' sites (former industrial or commercial sites) over green belt sites. Again, the result was a restriction of housing supply: brownfield sites are relatively few in number, and they are not necessarily located in areas where people want to live.

Of course, there is a debate to be had about how much of the UK's countryside we should turn into housing estates. But the issue is not as clear cut as most people realise. For instance, green belt areas, which mostly comprise farmland, are not on the same level of beauty as National Parks. Just because most people (myself included) would want to keep National Parks undeveloped, this doesn't mean that some green belt areas wouldn't be worth developing. The truth is, it's not as though we're overrun with urban areas in this country. One authoritative study found that the proportion of urban land in the UK is around 8%, a figure lower than that of the Netherlands (15%), Belgium (14.6%) and Denmark (9%). And it's not as though building in the countryside is always less environmentally friendly than urban building. Cities with plenty of gardens can be more biodiverse than farmland, with its agricultural uniformity. Moreover, it's not as though building on green belts would represent a radical change in our national agricultural policy; the UK is already a net importer of food, and has been since 1846. All of these facts need to be part of a sensible debate. What is not debatable is the fact that the green belt policy has acted like a restraining belt on the UK's housing supply.

In fact, green belts are the tip of a massive iceberg of obstructive governance in the housing sector. Since the Second World War, the government has restricted not just the space in which homes can be built, but the physical character of the homes themselves. And, as ever, this has been true not only of government-built housing but of privately built housing. In the 1960s, national building regulations came into force for the first time, thereby imposing legal restrictions on the way in which all new buildings were designed, constructed and altered. These regulations, which have impacted on architects, builders and homeowners, have been updated and extended many times. Recently, numerous updates have sought to make buildings more environmentally friendly. Further updates have emanated from the EU. By means of this expanding system of building regulations, the government has been shaping the character of all the homes built in Britain for half a century.

For the better? Not everyone is wholly convinced. In 2015, Conservative leader David Cameron was elected as Prime Minister. One of his campaign promises was that he would oversee a 'bonfire of the regulations', including 100 building regulations that, he insisted, were needlessly limiting the activities of housebuilders. I cannot claim to be an expert in these matters, so I asked a friend of mine, a retired builder, what he thought of the building regulations system. He replied that, although he agreed there should be some regulations and some level of oversight, the system had often "frustrated" him. He recounted how inspectors would turn up to scrutinise his work at regular intervals during a build. Some of the inspectors were "22-year-olds with a clip board". Another was "an ex bank manager who had done a year-long course on building inspection". The problem, obviously, was that inspectors like these had scant experience of the building trade. They were functionaries, box tickers, who were adding little of value to the process. As a result, the inspectors often insisted on measures that were legally necessary but, from a practical point of view, ridiculously unnecessary. On one occasion, when my friend was constructing a small private house, the inspector forced him to dig a foundation trench that was so deep and wide "you could have landed a Concorde on it". Naturally, unnecessary measures such as these take time and cost money, which further drives up house prices.

Better safe than sorry, you might argue. But actually, my friend argued, the building regulations system is no guarantor of safety. He explained that the box-ticking mindset of the inspectors, combined with their inexperience, often meant that they displayed an alarming lack of responsibility. If a project checked out legalistically then the inspectors were usually satisfied because "their arses were covered", even on occasions when an experienced builder might have flagged up concerns. For instance, my friend told me about a new local development, a housing estate, that was built on a flood plain. As a knowledgeable bystander, he could see that there were potential issues with flooding on the estate – and he turned out to be right. But the inspectors had blithely waved the project through. Sometimes, my friend hinted, the irrespon-sibility of the inspectors bordered on corruption. Questionable new developments were given the green light on the proviso that the builders would include, say, "a little kiddics' playground", or some other public amenity, in the final layout. In the public sector, image is everything; the prize of a virtuous-sounding new playground on a planner's CV can mask all manner of real-world failings. Indeed, a few years ago, this kind of agenda-driven irresponsibility led to disaster when the Grenfell Tower, a high-rise residential block owned and built by the London Borough of Kensington and Chelsea, burnt to the ground with at least 71 people inside it. The tower was clad with a combustible outer shell that was designed to make the building more energy efficient – in other words, more environmentally friendly. A nice idea. A horrible execution.

You don't need to be an expert builder to be sceptical about the current system of building regulations. All around us, all the time, there are millions of obvious counterarguments to the idea that such a system is necessary, at least in its current, ideologically exuberant form. I am talking, of course, about the millions of homes that were built in Britain before national building regulations were introduced. On the whole, Britain's older housing stock is not only beautiful but – by definition – sturdy and enduring. In particular, homes that were built in the Victorian era, a time renowned for its architectural flair and engineering skill, are today among the most desirable in the country. Even the quirks of Britain's older homes, the nooks and crannies, the odd-shaped rooms and low ceilings – quirks that today would be ironed out by building regulations – are much appreciated by homebuyers. One of the craziest ironies of the current inspection regime is that it is passionately supported by left-wingers many of whom themselves live in characterful old houses that predated the first national building regulations. In other words, these left-wingers, by their own choices, disprove the idea that only the government can ensure that adequate housing gets built. Indeed, many of these left-wingers live in the kinds of Victorian terraces that were considered 'slums' by the earliest – and least severe – of the UK's regulatory standards. People in glass houses shouldn't throw stones – and people in entrepreneurially constructed old houses shouldn't force other people to live in government-regulated dwellings.

After all, it's not as though all builders are cowboys. Far from it. Most builders are professionals who take personal pride in their work. And the few who are cowboys end up with a bad reputation and no customers (unless those customers happen to be local authorities that prioritise ideology over results). Giving builders more freedom to get on with their jobs would free up the market to weed out the cowboys, a task that the market excels at. In contrast, giving free reign to meddling bureaucrats, who think they know better than experienced builders how to build safely, and who think they know best what customers want from builders, is a recipe for failure.

Recently, a think tank called the Adam Smith Institute published an essay entitled 'Britain Needs More Slums'. The author, Theo Clifford, received death threats from angry socialists. But his proposal was essentially sound, despite his provocative use of the word 'slums'. In this context, a slum simply means a home that is designed and built by professionals not to satisfy government criteria but to satisfy *customers*. A slum could mean a 'Bed in a Shed', like the one I was kicked out of in Cambridge – a decent enough home for the right person. Or a slum could mean a home that is too small to fulfil government size standards but is nonetheless acceptable to customers. Clifford recounts how, a few years ago, the Mayor of

London had to intervene to allow the construction of a block of 'micro-flats' which, despite being worth up to £231,000 each, contravened various building regulations. It's a ludicrous situation when the government has to intervene to stop the government from intervening. Less government intervention is the obvious answer.

The obstructiveness of the current planning system is legendary. I'm sure you know someone – maybe you are someone – who has had to jump exhaustingly, expensively, through an epic series of regulatory hoops in order to get permission to build or extend a house. Horror stories abound, like the tale of Gerald Ringe, a man who purchased a desecrated chapel in a village in a green belt area of Essex. Ringe was intending to turn the chapel into a home, but 14 years later, having spent over £8000 on numerous planning applications and appeals, he gave up, because he still hadn't been given planning permission. The Council was quibbling over such matters as the loss of hedgerows, a loss which would supposedly be 'detrimental to the street scene' (actually the hedgerows were brambles). Indeed, the difficulties involved in getting planning permission are not just anecdotal or confined to controversial cases. Land prices reflect these difficulties. In the early twentieth century, land values in Britain remained more or less constant, but they started to climb after the Town and Country Planning Act was passed, as the price of land with planning permission increased compared to the price of land without such permission. The Valuation Office has calculated that agricultural land in England today is worth on average £21,000 per hectare, while land with planning permission for housing is worth on average £6 million per hectare. That's a heck of a surcharge for pointless governance.

Meanwhile, there are other expenses involved in obtaining and living in a home in Britain. The UK has the highest property taxes (measured as a proportion of the government's total tax takings) in the developed world. These property taxes include council tax, stamp duty, inheritance tax, planning gain tax, capital gains tax, and taxes on developers. The idea of imposing heavy taxes on a resource that is in short supply is ridiculous beyond belief. One of the oldest rules of governance is that if you want to discourage something, tax it. A good example of this rule in action is the government's recent tax on sugary drinks, a tax that was designed to tackle obesity. With the government levying heavy taxes on homes, no wonder homes are so thin on the ground, in every sense.

By way of the government's stringent planning system and swingeing property taxes, British citizens are being forced to pay for their own insecurity. This wasn't what the post-war socialists promised. They promised a more rational use of land in Britain. They promised homes for everyone. But how could they ever have delivered on these arrogant promises? How could a bunch of bureaucrats, even with their targets and inspections, ever have known how many homes were needed, what kind of homes were needed, where these homes were needed, and by whom?

Anyone who knows how much the poor have suffered under socialism throughout history and throughout the world ought not to be surprised by the impact of 70 years of socialist housing policies in the UK. Socialism specialises in creating shortages – especially shortages that hurt the poor – all the better to justify more socialism. Indeed, the long-term decline in government housebuilding in the UK has hurt the poorest of the poor, because government homes are earmarked for the most incapable and vulnerable members of society. The decline started in the early 1970s, continued up to the present, and spanned successive Labour and Conservative governments, the common thread being the Town and Country Planning Act – a textbook socialist policy. It is hard to make a case that public money wasn't available for building social housing during this period. Public spending rose continually, trebling in real terms. Welfare spending rose too, from tens of billions annually at the end of the Second World War to over £200 billion annually today (again in real terms). By 2015, the amount of money the UK was spending on welfare accounted for a mind-boggling 7% of the world's total welfare spend. Moreover, over the last few decades, government borrowing has mushroomed. Yet the more the government has grown, and grown richer, and the more largesse it has shown, the more the government has failed to fulfil its self-appointed role of providing housing for the people who need it most.

Of course, to some extent the growth in welfare spending can be considered a symptom of the housing crisis. But only to some extent. The housing crisis didn't force huge numbers of people to become single mothers, alcoholics, drug abusers or benefit fraudsters. Nor did the housing crisis force the government to import huge numbers of benefits claimants via mass immigration. Indeed, the growth in welfare spending can also be considered a *cause* of the housing crisis. Thanks to the government's deep pockets, housing benefit claimants have been able to compete for houses on the open market. Since 2007, local authorities have handed out a 'Local Housing Allowance' to claimants – a weekly subvention based on the cost of renting in the local area. Initially, the allowance was pegged to the median local rent, and, naturally, claimants in the most affluent parts of the country eagerly took advantage of this opportunity. One Afghan family was found living in a £1.2 million mansion, drawing on around £3000 of public money each week. Later, the allowance was pegged to the thirtieth percentile of the local rent. But this didn't stop landlords from continuing to take advantage of the scheme, by raising their rents in line with the spending power of council tenants, thus driving up prices for everyone.

Over the last few decades, not only has the government failed in its responsibility to provide enough social housing, but it has increasingly farmed out much of that responsibility to organisations known as 'housing associations'. Dating back to the late nineteenth century, housing associations started out as charities or community organisations. They built homes and rented them to local people who needed assistance. However, with the growth of the welfare state (which came at the expense of the voluntary sector), and with the growth of the government's tendency to use private contractors, most housing associations evolved into profit-making enterprises part-funded by public money. The theory behind this hybrid status (a theory promulgated by both the Conservatives and New Labour) was that public-private organisations would combine the best features of socialism and capitalism, respectively. Unfortunately, the theory turned out to be diametrically false: public-private organisations ended up combining the *worst* features of socialism and capitalism, respectively, namely, public sector inefficiency and corporate greed. One survey by Channel 4 found that in order to build a three-bedroom home, housing associations spend an average of £150,000, compared to private builders who spend just £90,000. From 2000 to 2014, Britain's 1500 housing associations between them built only 26,000 homes per year, despite being awarded £62 billion in government funding during that period. Nonetheless, many of the Chief Executives of these housing associations are being rewarded with enormous salaries. In 2015/16, the most highly paid CEO, David Cowans of Places for People, earned £528,870 per year; nine of the top ten received salaries in excess of £250,000.

Over the last several decades, private developers have built way more homes than the government and housing associations combined. But this doesn't mean that the private sector hasn't contributed to rising house prices. It has, in many ways. For instance, you've probably heard of the much-maligned practice of 'landbanking', whereby developers make a profit out of land without building any houses on it. The developers buy the land then sit back and wait for it to increase in value before selling it on. In 2015, the *Guardian* reported that Britain's four biggest housebuilders were sitting on plots of land with planning permission to build more than 600,000 homes. These theoretical houses are boosting the prices of actual houses.

The housing crisis has also been exacerbated by a 30% rise since the year 2000 in the proportion of people who own a second home. One in ten UK adults now owns a second home, while four in ten adults own no property at all. Moreover, rich people from overseas have also played a role in the crisis. Researchers at King's College London estimated that foreign investment has added a whopping 20% to UK house prices over the past 15 years.

Another major factor that has bumped up house prices in the UK is the growth of the 'buy-to-let' market. Several decades ago buyers found it difficult to get a loan if they were purchasing a property intended for the rental market. But in 1996 the Association of Residential Lettings joined up with a group of lenders to launch 'buy-to-let mortgages', whereby investors could borrow on similar terms to owner-occupiers. Over the next two decades, the number of private landlords in the UK rocketed from tens of thousands to a record 2.5 million at the time of writing. Between them, these landlords own around five million rental properties. One government report has estimated that the growth of buy-to-let mortgages may have added 'up to 7%' to house prices. Property investors have been motivated not just by profits but by a recent spate of television programmes, books, newspaper articles and websites, all of which have added a touch of glamour to being a landlord – a far cry from the whiff of social disapproval that accompanied private landlords prior to the expansion of the buy-to-let market. Indeed, the phrase 'property investor' doesn't do justice to how popular the idea of being a landlord has become. These days, when people buy a new home they often rent out their old home rather than sell it; property portfolios, it seems, are now considered a natural form of human expression.

In all of this, a sort of collective mania has been at work. House price growth in the UK is an example of what economists call a 'bubble'. An economic bubble occurs when people invest in a particular resource purely because they believe that other people are investing in that resource. The resource becomes more expensive not for any intrinsic reason but because all the investors are confident that they and other buyers will keep bidding the prices up. The private sector's contribution to the housing crisis can largely be attributed to a housing bubble. Landbankers, foreign investors, buy-to-let landlords, and other casual 'property investors' – all these financial speculators have been, to some degree, motivated by each other. If they were all to desist from speculating on the housing market, they'd all be less incentivised to speculate on the housing the market.

But note: the housing crisis isn't happening solely because of a housing bubble. The bubble itself has a deeper cause, namely, the enduring combination of low supply and high demand in the market. If speculators weren't confident that supply wasn't going to rise and demand wasn't going to fall, the bubble would never have got started, and it probably wouldn't carry on growing. Moreover, as we have seen, chronically low supply and high demand themselves have a deeper cause: government control. The Town and Country Planning Act, in its various iterations, has throttled the supply of housing, while the policy of mass immigration has led to a relentless increase in the demand for housing. In turn, these disastrous government policies likewise have a deeper cause. If the housing crisis is a perfect storm – a storm of speculative exuberance superimposed upon layers of bad governance – then at the epicentre of this storm is a dominant force: the ideology of socialism. Socialists were responsible for enshrining in law in 1947 the dismal idea that the housing market could be planned by bureaucrats. Socialists were responsible for relaxing the UK's borders in 1997, leading to a huge influx of migrants. And – although the recent surge in immigration was partly the result of EU free movement – socialists have, more than anyone else, been responsible for rancorously silencing debate on the issue of mass immigration.

Alas, the storm may be about to become even more perfect. A recent survey found that more people in Britain have a 'favourable' view of socialism than of capitalism (36% versus 32%), and, conversely, more people have an 'unfavourable' view of capitalism than of socialism (39% versus 32%). This last statistic is so alarming it deserves to be restated baldly: *socialism, despite being one the most destructive and murderous ideologies in history, is out of favour with only one in three people in Britain today*. Worse, the survey found that the only age group in which a majority of respondents view socialism unfavourably is the over 60s; most people younger than 60 are woefully unaware of the dangers of socialism.

These trends were manifested in the 2017 general election, when Jeremy Corbyn, probably the most far-left leader in Labour's history, gained 40% of the overall vote, narrowly missing out on victory. Younger voters in the election were more likely to vote Labour, with almost two thirds under the age of 30 doing so. The man they voted for, Corbyn, has a lot of respect for Karl Marx (whom he has called a "great economist") and almost nothing good to say about capitalism, the most powerful poverty-reduction system in history. In a recent BBC interview, when asked "is there anything that capitalism gets right?", Corbyn declined to give an example, responding: "Well, it's a system that's evolved, it's a system that's there..." When the interviewer repeated the question, Corbyn added: "Well, it does invest, mainly for its own benefit, but it does of course get challenged..."

As for Labour's Shadow Chancellor, John McDonnell, at least he is more forthright in his frightening views. When asked, in a BBC interview, if "the overthrow of capitalism" is his "job", he replied "yes, it is", adding that socialism means "transforming the economy" in a way that "radically challenges the system as it now is". Speaking at a recent conference on Marx, he declared that "Marxism is about the freedom of spirit, the development of life chances", and is "a force for change today". Most worryingly of all, McDonnell has also declared: "I want to be in a situation where no Tory MP can travel anywhere in the country or show their face anywhere in public without being challenged, without direct action"; Tory MPs, he surmised, are "social criminals". To put these comments in perspective, imagine if McDonnell was a *fascist* who dubbed his parliamentary opponents "social criminals" and called for them to be hounded by his supporters. It's all too easy to imagine; or maybe it needs no imagination at all.

Certainly, no imagination is needed to correctly predict how a Labour Party led by Corbyn and McDonnell will deal with the housing crisis: cackhandedly. The 'Secure Homes for All' section of Labour's manifesto is full of hackneyed promises. There are promises of bureaucratic measures: 'we will establish a new Department for Housing to focus on tackling the crisis'; 'we will overhaul the Homes and Communities Agency to be Labour's housing delivery body'; 'we will make the building of new homes, including council homes, a priority through our National Transformation Fund, as part of a joined-up industrial and skills strategy'. There are promises of restrictive planning: 'we will prioritise brownfield sites and protect the green belt'; 'we will consult on new rules on minimum space standards... and on new modern standards for building "zero carbon homes"'.

And there is even a promise of resurrecting a socialist housing policy from the 1960s, namely, 'controls on rent rises'. Rent controls – government restrictions on rents or on rent increases – have been shunned by every government for half a century in the UK. Among economists, the consensus is that rent controls discourage private investment in new housing, and therefore restrict supply, thus hurting the poor the most. Corbyn has stated that "rent controls exist in many cities across the world and I want our cities to have those powers too". But, as Anthony Breach explains, you cannot solve the housing problems of a city by forcibly reducing its rents:

All the international evidence shows that rent controls divide renters into the privileged and the outsiders. Those already in rented flats when controls are introduced do well, but the city's young people and migrants from the rest of the country and abroad are penalised as they need the new homes that are not being built.

You can't fix a housing bubble by arbitrarily putting a

finger on the scales of housing costs.

Of course, being socialists, Corbyn and his supporters are confident that if they get into power they will be able to harass the private sector with one hand while building a better world with the other. Labour's manifesto states that 'we will be building at least 100,000 council and housing association homes a year for genuinely affordable rent or sale'. I wouldn't bet on it. And, anyway, if mass immigration were to continue at its present rate, these new homes would account for less than half of annual net migration – in which case the housing crisis would intensify even if Labour's own best case scenario comes to pass. Given this, which way do you think Labour MPs voted in the EU referendum? Well, here's the kicker: a survey of MPs prior to the EU referendum found that, out of 218 Labour MPs, *only 11 planned to vote Leave*. The Labour Party isn't serious about solving the housing crisis. Einstein's definition of insanity springs to mind: doing the same thing over and over and expecting a different result.

Sane or not, the socialists who currently dominate the Labour Party are guilty of contempt – contempt for the majority of people. Most people don't want to 'overthrow capitalism'. Quite the contrary: they want to work in a career of their choosing, make money, accumulate possessions, be generous to their families and communities, and be able to call somewhere 'home', preferably somewhere that they own. In every sense of the word 'property', most people ideally don't want their property to be owned by the government, because they know that their ability to dispose of their own property enhances their freedom.

Most people also feel this way in regard to their

country. I am often asked why I support capitalism but I don't support EU free movement. The reason is this: whereas money and goods can and should move freely throughout the world, because money and goods have no sense of place, most people – especially those who share a language – do have a sense of place, including a sense of nationhood. Nebulously, and tenuously, but tenaciously, most people sense that their country is their property. Accordingly, a country should never be the plaything of a government; a country should never be considered a resource to be disposed of against the will of the people who live there. Even more emphatically, a country should never be the plaything of foreign unelected bureaucrats. The EU's attempt to rebalance the economies of Europe by encouraging mass migration from lands scarred by communism into lands historically nourished by democracy is itself a form of socialism, an extreme form of it – an attempt to expropriate and exploit property on the largest possible scale. And, more generally, the left's attempt to impose global mass migration on the UK is part of the same pattern: contempt for the idea that a country belongs to its inhabitants, and therefore contempt for those inhabitants.

If we want a planning system that doesn't debase the idea of private property, and a migration system that doesn't debase the idea that a country is owned by its inhabitants, we urgently need to challenge socialist ideology. Alas, socialism has become almost unchallengeable in intellectual life in Britain. Universities have become bastions of left-wing thought, with one report estimating that fewer than 12% of academics today are conservatives. On campuses, aggressive protestors are shouting down critics of socialism –

whether students, lecturers or outside speakers. Many of these protestors are also shouting down critics of the EU. In turn, the UK's wider culture is increasingly being shaped by all this intolerant, lefty sloganeering. Millions of socialism-indoctrinated students have graduated into culturally influential jobs, for instance in the media, the arts, education, the legal profession, and of course the government. Throughout the country, the truth about the housing crisis is being obscured by a miasma of socialist lies.

Socialism's contribution to the housing crisis is so deep, intense and pervasive that I can sympathise with people who pine for a socialist solution to the crisis. I can sympathise with the hopelessly hopeful young people who sing "Ooooh Jeremy Corbyn" at pop concerts, or the hardworking poor people who assume that only the government can build them the home that they can't afford through their own efforts, or indeed the lazy welfare miscreants who bury their heads in drugs and alcohol and domestic strife while angrily demanding that the government feeds, clothes and houses them.

I can sympathise with all these people, because, like believers in God, they seem to be suffering from a kind of Stockholm Syndrome. After all, socialist leaders throughout history have promised to deliver solutions to problems that were caused by socialism. To be a follower of such a leader makes a sort of perverted sense when the leader is powerful enough to have caused the problems in the first place; a hand that takes food from you is also a hand that could feed you.

Consider how this dynamic works in the housing market. Imagine if you were imprisoned in a basement, held captive by an irascible, irrational bully.

Imagine if you had never seen the outside world, and no one had ever told you much about it. Imagine if you wanted more from your life than this chronic humiliation. Imagine, indeed, if you wanted to live upstairs, like your captor, amid the luxury you had glimpsed through cracks in the floorboards. Imagine if you felt your only hope was to beg your captor to indulge your demands, such was his commanding influence over your life and your prospects. This is the position that many British people, especially young people, find themselves in today – mentally and emotionally, if not literally. Socialism has such a merciless grip on the housing prospects of so many Britons, one can almost forgive them for assuming that only socialism can save them from humiliation.

If only these captives knew the truth – that they could escape into a big wide world, a world where freedom reigns, a world where people can dream their own dreams, and *build* their own dreams, instead of living in a nightmare dreamt up by other people. If only these captives knew that they *should* know. An escape route is staring them in the face. The basement contains an unlocked door upon which a sign hangs. The sign is emblazoned with a skull and crossbones along with an intimidating slogan: 'WARNING – CAPITALISM – DO NOT PROCEED!' If only the captives would walk out of that door, whereupon they would discover that they had been duped. Together they could bring about change; they could embrace capitalism; they could demand that Britain's socialist simulacrum of a housing market be replaced with a real housing market.

There is something especially poignant about the fact that so many young people today are using the internet to express their ardour for socialism and their disgust for capitalism. Social media platforms such as Twitter and facebook are overrun by angry keyboard warriors who are ganging up on anyone who dares to challenge the narrative peddled by the left. The irony is, the angry socialists who are prosecuting these campaigns of online intimidation are using modern technology that was forged in the crucible of capitalism. The astonishing rise of information technology over the last few decades exemplifies what is achievable, in a short space of time, when private companies are allowed to do what they do best: profiting from the manufacture of innovative products that people can afford to buy. And it's not just information technology that has blossomed under the free market. Capitalism has lowered the costs, and increased the quality, of almost everything we buy today, including food, light, energy, transportation, plumbing, and even housing – or rather, in the UK housing *would* be cheaper than ever if its value weren't arbitrarily being boosted by government-led market distortions. If only the electorate would demand a capitalism-led housing market.

For the time being, the EU referendum has shown that the UK population has demanded to be free from mass immigration – and that's a good start. But the reaction of many young people to the referendum result was no less poignant than their online campaigning for socialism. The demographic breakdown of the result showed that older voters were more likely to vote Leave, with 64% of people aged 65 or over doing so, compared to just 29% of voters aged 18-24. In reaction, many young Remainers were outraged, insisting that their future had been stolen from them by the older generation. Some young Remainers went as far as to say, in effect: Britain's older voters will be dead soon, so we shouldn't care what they think. Never mind the terrible disrespect involved in this verdict – the disrespect for wisdom, and the disrespect for the many Leavers who, having lived through the Second World War, knew a thing or two about what is in Britain's interests when it comes to Europe. The worst thing about the angry reaction of many young Remainers to the referendum result was that they were looking a gift horse in the mouth. Blinded by socialist propaganda, they failed to see the obvious: that a reduction in housing demand thanks to a reduction in immigration would be a shot in the arm for their housing prospects.

Of course, if I am right that socialism, with its accompanying support for excessive regulation and mass immigration, has been the main cause of the housing crisis, then there's another reason to sympathise with young people who support socialism: *successive conservative governments have given conservatism a bad name by perpetuating socialist housing policies and calling them 'conservative'*. This is the absolute worst thing conservatives could have done: they have acted like trained doctors who practise homeopathy and call it evidenced-based medicine; they have given genuinely effective measures a bad name.

Admittedly, not everything the Conservatives have done in housing has been misguided or ineffective. In 1980, Conservative Prime Minister Margaret Thatcher oversaw a huge expansion of the 'Right to Buy' scheme, whereby council housing tenants could purchase their homes from the government at a heavily discounted price. By 1987, more than a million people had taken advantage of the scheme and become homeowners. This amounted to both an increase in the freedom of the UK population and an increase in the size of the public purse. But there's the rub: Thatcher's reputation as a supporter of free market economics is not entirely merited. Public spending rose in real terms under her administration. And her obsession with creating 'efficient' government services achieved little other than an acceleration of the post-war trend towards Soviet-style management in the public sector. Bureaucratic strategies, plans and targets proliferated under the Iron Lady.

And, all the while, bureaucratic strategies, plans and targets continued to dominate the housing sector. Indeed, this was true not just of Thatcher's government but of every Conservative government since the Second World War. The Conservatives' overall housing policy in the last 70 years has been a case of tweaking rather than replacing the radical system of housing control implemented by the post-war socialists. Despite throwing a few regulations onto the bonfire, no Conservative government has been willing to renounce (or even denounce) the fundamental conceit underpinning the UK's housing system: the idea that the government should get to dictate to private landowners what they are allowed to build on their own land. On the contrary, the more the housing crisis has intensified, the more the Conservatives have doubled down on this fundamental conceit, in word and in deed. Just like their Labour counterparts, the Conservatives have piously promised that in government they would 'take action' and 'do more' to solve the housing crisis – they would 'deliver' more housing

– whereas, in fact, if they really wanted to see the crisis solved, they should have promised to do less in government, by repealing or radically attenuating the Town and Country Planning Act, thus allowing free people to solve the crisis on their own.

In government, the Tories have even had the cheek to offer taxpayers 'help' with buying a house. Carried over from the 'Low Cost Home Ownership' scheme run by the previous Labour administration, the 'Help to Buy' scheme (which has recently been scrapped) allowed people to purchase a house at an affordable price, because a share of the equity was owned by the government, with the purchaser buying back that share over time. Sounds helpful, right? Well, not really. Housing is unaffordable because the government has made it unaffordable. Being offered 'Help to Buy' by the government is like being offered a loan by someone who has just mugged you. And, worse, George Osborne, the Chancellor who rolled out the scheme, acknowledged that it might serve to inflate houses prices (which it did, while also boosting the profits of private builders, who simply put up their prices to match the superior spending power of government-funded buyers). So, in privileging a few buyers and builders, the government intensified the housing crisis for everyone else, and added some more bureaucracy into the mix. In the grand scheme of things, the 'Help to Buy' scheme has been no more helpful than rent controls.

And, of course, another area in which the Tories have failed miserably is immigration policy. The Conservatives signed the Maastricht Treaty which led to mass immigration from Europe. They then failed to stem the wider flow of mass immigration that began under New Labour. Perhaps you might argue that the Tories deserve credit for at least being willing to *talk about* controlling immigration. But this talk has been insincere. Without walking the walk – that is, without controlling the UK's borders – the Conservatives have only succeeded in making themselves sound ineffectual and crass.

As for the complex relationship between the Conservatives and the EU, I will refrain from opening that can of worms here. Suffice it to say that many conservatives who supported the EU and free movement did so for laudable reasons, namely, to promote international trade and cooperation (and the same goes, no doubt, for some left-wing Remainers). Moreover, most of the conservatives who voted Remain wanted to reform the EU – they were so-called 'reluctant Remainers'. But the fact is, reluctant Remainers gambled with the future of British poor people. In this way, many Tories acted like reckless socialists while calling the policy conservatism.

By calling themselves capitalists but governing as socialists, the Conservatives have helped trash the reputation of capitalism. In an overcrowded UK where homes are in short supply, capitalism is alive and kicking, but it is kicking a little harder than usual. There is a harshness, a ruthlessness, a cynicism prevalent in Britain nowadays. When socialists complain about the 'greed' manifest in British society, they are right, but not because commerce is greedy, but because Britain is a country in which people are becoming increasingly desperate. Britons are pushing and shoving like peasants queueing to buy bread in the USSR; in effect, vast swathes of the UK population are permanently living in a long queue for housing.

The worst thing is, the Tories had ample warning that capitalism was in danger of being tarnished both in image and in reality by the effects of socialism. Tony Blair had a reputation as a 'capitalist', despite overseeing massive increases in public spending and in immigration. Following New Labour, the Tories should have drawn a line under this fake version of capitalism, by saying "*that* wasn't capitalism, *but this is*" and then proceeding to govern as conservatives. Instead, they willingly lived up to their role as scapegoats. They willingly maintained public spending and immigration at the astronomical levels reached under New Labour, thus letting capitalism continue to take the blame for the failings of socialism – not just in housing but in the health service, schools, universities, and countless other areas of the economy. Bizarrely, the Conservatives have governed as fall guys.

Why have the Tories pandered so abjectly to socialism, even when in government? I suppose power has something to do with it. All public servants face a constant temptation to extend or at least maintain their power rather than relinquish it. Presumably, working for the state can turn a weak-willed conservative into a determined statist. Relatedly, another factor that has caused conservatives to pander to socialism is their desire to impress the electorate. Announcing "When in government, we will do less for you" is guaranteed to alienate huge numbers of voters, especially those who are dependents or employees of the state. As a result, the Conservatives have often promised – and done – more in government than the preceding administration. At the same time, the Conservatives have also been encouraged by their own supporters to enact non-conservative policies. This is true specifically in the area of housing. People who own property tend to support restrictive government planning, in order to maintain or increase the value of their property. Ironically, socialists who favour government intervention in the housing market are singing from the same hymn sheet as their arch-enemies, namely, rich homeowners and property market speculators.

I also wonder whether many conservatives in government have been shaped by another force that hasn't been entirely conducive to genuine conservatism: Christianity. I say 'entirely' because no doubt many Christians are ardent champions of conservative values: values such as personal responsibility, economic freedom, communitarianism, charity, financial prudence and democracy. But, at the same time, many Christians are sympathetic to socialist values. Indeed, the leaders of both the Church of England and the Catholic Church have recently displayed socialist leanings. The Archbishop of Canterbury, Justin Welby, has called for tax rises, argued for a "purposeful and active state", criticised the Tories' benefit reforms, described zero-hours contracts as "evil", lavishly praised unions, and insisted euphemistically that Jesus himself was "highly political", because "he told the rich [...] they would face woes". Meanwhile, Pope Francis has been even more florid in his left-wing rhetoric, insisting: "Once capital becomes an idol and guides people's decisions, once greed for money presides over the entire socioeconomic system, it ruins society, it condemns and enslaves men and women, it destroys human fraternity, it sets people against one another."

At first sight, this schism between conservative and socialist tendencies within Christianity seems surprising. But when you consider the theological basis of

Christianity, the schism makes more sense. Christian theologians tell us that God gave us free will and therefore responsibility for our lives; this aspect of Christianity fits neatly with conservatism. However, the same theologians also tell us that God commanded us to use our free will to serve him; we are part of his overall plan for humanity; we are all united as God's servants. Obviously, the precise nature of God's plan is open to interpretation, but the very idea of such a plan sounds suspiciously like socialism. Both Christianity and socialism implore us to live our lives in accordance with a benevolent plan designed by a higher authority. Both encourage us to experience fellowship in pursuit of this plan, a plan which is 'bigger than ourselves'. Both warn us not to stray from the plan by pursuing material gain, or 'mammon'. Both, in effect, offer us salvation, whether in the form of heaven or utopia; we will be saved, so it goes, only if we conform. Indeed, this promise of salvation is what makes both socialism and Christianity (and indeed all theistic religions) examples of a Stockholm Syndrome – that is, a psychological complex in which we believe that our suffering can be relieved by the same domineering force that caused our suffering in the first place. Just as socialist bureaucrats supposedly can save us from the chaos wrought by socialism, God supposedly can save us from his own creation.

Hence, Christianity's leftist streak is unsurprising when you consider the doctrinal and psychological affinities between Christianity and socialism. Though there are undoubtedly many Christians who see God's plan as avowedly *not* a socialist plan, there are many others – including highly influential others – who are more sympathetic to socialism; indeed, the current

Leader of the Conservative Party, Theresa May, is arguably one such Christian. I suppose that somewhere in the middle there are Christians who are pulled away from or towards a socialist interpretation of God's plan depending on the circumstances. There are probably many such impressionable believers in the Conservative Party; that is, there are many conservatives who champion human freedom but will happily accept a socialist interpretation of God's plan when placed under electoral, moral or religious pressure to do so. Under growing pressure from socialists, such impressionable Christian conservatives, I suspect, have contributed to conservatism's leftward lurch in the UK.

In this connection, I cannot help but think of my landlady in Cambridge, with her strange blend of views. On one hand, she was an ardent conservative, a committed believer in personal responsibility. On the other hand, she was a committed believer in the mystical idea that all human behaviour emanates from a loving universal spirit in which all individuals merge and disappear. In the end, just like my landlady, many conservative Christians display traces of the same kind of authoritarianism that theism and socialism have always displayed. Those who try to convince us that we belong to an all-powerful loving community also try to make us conform.

Still, I don't want to be too harsh on conservatives, most of whom are staunch opponents of socialism, and most of whom receive a ton of abuse for their efforts. Indeed, recently there has been a suggestion that, even with the best will in the world, conservatives would have struggled to arrest the relentless advance of socialism in the UK. Steve Hilton, who was an advisor to Conservative Prime Minister David Cameron, explained how Cameron's government struggled to keep a grip on the public sector. Here is Hilton reminiscing about his time in power:

> Very often you'll wake up in the morning and hear on the radio or the news or see something in the newspapers about something the government is doing... And you think, 'Well, hang on a second – it's not just that we didn't know it was happening, but we don't even agree with it!' The government can be doing things... and we don't agree with it? How can that be?

He continues:

> [O]nly 30% of what the government is doing is actually delivering what we're supposed to be doing. It just shows you the scale of what you're up against... when I found that out, that was pretty horrific.

His conclusion: 'the bureaucracy masters the politicians.'

It is tempting to attribute this kind of statement to weakness. But today, in the US, even the unbullyable Donald Trump is struggling to master the bureaucrats in Washington and the rest of the country. His attempt to 'drain the swamp' has been met with an unbelievably angry response from his political opponents, many of whom have a vested interested in big government.

Unfortunately, thwarting conservative governance even when conservatives are in power has been a longstanding tactic of the left. In Germany half a century ago, student activist Rudi Dutschke coined the phrase 'the long march through the institutions'. His idea was that socialists should try to foment a revolution not by sudden violent means but by gradually infiltrating organisations that play a large role in shaping the public's behaviour and opinions. Throughout the developed world, Dutschke's vivid rallying cry was eagerly adopted in the 1960s by the 'counter-culture' generation. With their political views based on a lazy blend of mysticism, socialism and drug-induced unrealism, these hippies spent the next half century not only marching through the institutions but setting up camp in them. Today, the infiltrated institutions include schools, universities, government departments, local authorities, immigration authorities, the media, the legal profession, big businesses, charities, religious organisations, political parties, and even international bodies such as the EU and the UN. You can hardly find a single institution anywhere these days in which you won't be (at best) frowned upon for expressing conservative views.

With the UK's institutions being integral to its economy, there is a serious risk of economic collapse in the UK. Upon such a collapse, the revolutionaries will have achieved their aim: destroying capitalism and blaming it for its own downfall. In the face of this threat, there is no room for complacency. Sometimes a structure will collapse even though only one of its pillars has been fatally compromised. Of all the pillars of the UK's economy, the housing market is one of the most fundamental, and the most vulnerable. Since the Second World War, socialists have been applying relentless pressure to the housing market, by way of their roles in central government, local government and the public-private sector, and, more recently, by way of their legislative support for mass immigration. All the while, socialists have consolidated this pressure by using their roles within cultural institutions to aggressively champion socialist values. Indeed, you could argue that the housing market has already been destroyed, and the economy is already, as a result, broken. If that's true, Jeremy Corbyn and his comrades in the Labour Party have already won; they are a government in waiting.

The destructive effects of the left's long march though the institutions, and particularly its effects on the housing market, are nowhere more evident than in London, a city that could itself be described as a British 'institution'. Average house prices in the capital have reached a bewildering £500,000 in the last few years, making it the second most unaffordable city in the world (after Hong Kong), with the average wage in London around £30,000 per year. Moreover, for the last three years, London has been the most expensive city in Europe to rent in. Like most places in the country, the capital has suffered from a lack of housing supply (due to overregulation) and an increase in demand for housing (largely due to mass immigration). But in London the increase in demand has been exceptional. In 1991, the population of the capital was 6.4 million. By 2016, that figure had grown to 8.8 million. And by 2021, it is expected to have risen to 9.3 million. Today, at least 37% of the people living in London are foreign-born. That's around 3.32 million in total, of whom around a third are EU citizens. In 2015, two out of every three babies born in the capital had at least one foreign-born parent.

And, of course, London is also a magnet for British university graduates, almost a quarter of whom have been moving to the capital within six months of graduating. With increasing numbers of people having attended university over the last few decades, that's another significant influx.

London's graduates and immigrants have shaped the capital not only through their numerical presence but through their political tendencies. Having been indoctrinated at university, graduates tend to have leftist views, as do immigrants, especially those who are Muslims, of whom there are around a million today in the capital. Hence, left-leaning political views now predominate in London. In 2017, the Labour Party won 49 of the capital's 73 constituencies, gaining 54.5% of the total vote (compared to the Tories' 33.1%). In the EU referendum, almost 60% of Londoners voted Remain. And in 2016, Sadiq Kahn was the first ever Muslim to be elected Mayor of London, gaining almost 57% of the vote. With ongoing support for socialism and mass immigration implied by way of these results, many Londoners have, in effect, shown a preference for perpetuating their own housing crisis. Worse, the political tendencies of Londoners are bound to impact on the rest of the country given that the capital is the seat of the government as well as the UK's most culturally influential city.

Of course, not everyone in the UK agrees with the majority of Londoners. Throughout the rest of the UK there is a lot of scepticism, even defiance, towards the capital. Moreover, plenty of people from London don't agree with the majority in the capital. In recent years, these dissenting Londoners have been involved in a remarkable – but seldom remarked upon – phenomenon. From 2000 to 2013, 620,000 people who identified as 'white British' quit the capital. This was the equivalent of the entire population of Glasgow upping and leaving in a decade – an enormous, almost epoch-making demographic change.

The ugly phrase 'white flight' has been used to describe this exodus of white British people from London. However, I think focusing on the skin colour of the departees is unhelpful and misleading. The fact that they had white skin is incidental. Their skin colour points to a deeper fact, namely, that most of the departees were from communities with longstanding ties to London, communities of people who – for obvious historical reasons – happened to be white. The white departees did not leave *because* they were white, or *because* other Londoners were not white. They left for numerous reasons that had nothing to do with race. To describe these people as part of a 'white flight' is, in the end, to insinuate that their departure was racially motivated – and it was not.

So why did so many Londoners quit the capital? Undoubtedly, many of them left because they couldn't afford to buy a house in London, or couldn't even afford to rent there. As for the other reasons, we can speculate. Perhaps the departees didn't want to live in an overcrowded home – London's houses are twice as overcrowded as those of the rest of England. (In 2015, 26 people were found living in one three-bedroom home in East London). Perhaps the departees were also concerned about the impact of overcrowding on public services in the capital, including schools, the health service and social services, and the London Underground. Anyone who has ever walked down the street in London knows that the capital is bursting at the seams. Perhaps the departees were fed up of living in a city where life for so many people, graduates and immigrants alike, is transitory – a staging post where grim conditions are tolerated en route to a hoped-for better future. Perhaps the departees felt that their own present was being sacrificed on the altar of other people's futures. Perhaps the departees were fed up of listening to the sloganeering of left-wing university graduates, especially graduates who were able to sail clear of the housing crisis in their well-paid government jobs, even as those jobs helped perpetuate the crisis. Perhaps the departees were fed up of seeing welfare payments handed out to immigrants who had never paid into the system.

Perhaps the departees were disturbed by the cultural changes wrought by mass immigration in the capital. There are over 300 languages spoken in London today, making the capital the most linguistically diverse city in the world. Perhaps the departees wanted their children to be taught in a school where most of the children speak English as a first language. Perhaps the departees were concerned that, throughout the public sector in London, valuable resources are being spent on overcoming linguistic barriers. Perhaps the departees were disturbed by the lack of social cohesion in the capital. Multiculturalism, after all, has a dark side: people of different cultures often become strangers to each other. Londoners are increasingly atomised, or at best separated into cultural ghettos. Many of these hermetically sealed communities are at war with each other, with gang violence, including knife crime and acid attacks, rife in London. And, of course, Londoners live in constant fear of Islamic terrorism.

Amid all this social dysfunction and its frightening effects, it is hardly surprising that London has become a city in which alcohol and drugs are commonplace (especially with so many university graduates in town). Feeling insecure, many Londoners have turned to narcosis as the basis of their social lives.

Meanwhile, amid the profusion of new cultures in London, Britain's 'Western' values have increasingly fallen by the wayside. These universalist values – values of freedom, tolerance, secularism and democracy – could and should have been (and to some extent have been) a unifying force for all immigrants in the UK. But, sadly, some of the UK's immigrants have shunned the culture of their host country. And they have been encouraged to do so by socialists who have propagated the dismal and ludicrous idea that Western values are the oppressive values of white people. Perhaps the London departees were fed up of all this racist nonsense. Perhaps they wanted to live in a part of the country where Western values are still predominant and are still considered applicable to everyone, whatever their skin colour. It's a sad state of affairs for these Londoners, who are cultural refugees in their own country. It's even sadder when you consider the sacrifices that were made by Londoners during the Second World War. In huge numbers, at home and abroad, Londoners suffered and died to defend Western values against the racist socialism of the Nazis. And now the descendants of these Londoners are quitting their own city in droves, dismayed at the decline of Western values in London, a decline overseen by… racist socialists.

So much for London. It is not my home any more. It hasn't been my home for ten years. Looking back on this period, a period of chaos and conflict in my life, I realise now that I have to accept some share of responsibility for my own personal housing crisis. I should have fixed the door on my dad's van. I should have moved to Durham a long time ago. I should have tried harder to get along with people.

But when I think of all the arguments I have had, one thing stands out above all – how easily people take offence at the truth. Sadly, I suppose this book will offend some people, especially socialists – not because it is offensive, but because some people will aggressively choose to be offended. I suppose these people will hurl epithets at me for daring to discuss the undiscussable. And I suppose my own background won't provide much mitigation for me: technically, I am an immigrant too, having been born in Australia and brought to London as a baby, my mum being an Australian and my dad being a New Zealander. I suppose the offence-takers will, irrelevantly and illogically, call me a hypocrite. My message to these people is: *get real*. The housing crisis is happening primarily because of socialist planning policies that have discouraged the building of new homes, and because of a policy of mass immigration – implemented and fiercely backed by socialists – that has allowed far too many people to come to Britain.

"Get real" may sound like a strange conclusion for a book in which I have complained that the housing crisis has had a negative impact on creativity in the UK. Well, I've discovered over the years that people who face up to reality – whether artists, entrepreneurs, scientists, or none of the above – are the most creative people of all. Reality can be a cruel place; only human ingenuity and imagination can help us to deal with this world and thrive in it, and this is the only world we've got. If we want to solve the housing crisis – if we want to help people, especially young people, navigate the perfect storm that is currently raging throughout Britain – we need to unleash the creativity of capitalism; of architects and builders and financiers. We need to release Britain from the stultifying power of socialist governance. Above all, we need our intellectuals to show a bit of imagination, as per their job description. In doing so, they could inspire us all to get real. They could help us see past the slogans of socialism – the cognitive dead ends and conversation stoppers that, in the end, stop progress in its tracks.

Printed in Great Britain
by Amazon

66631891R00108